Will the Theologians Please Sit Down

David Bercot

SCROLL
PUBLISHING

Vision Publishers
PO Box 190
Harrisonburg, VA 22803
www.vision-publishers.com
ph. - 877.488.0901 • fax -540.437.1969
email - cs@vision-publishers.com
We Welcome Your Response!

Published by Scroll Publishing Company, P.O. Box 122, Amberson, PA 17210. (717) 349-7033. www.scrollpublishing.com

Write for a free catalog of our publications.

ISBN: 978-0-924722-24-0

The author wishes to express his deep appreciation and indebtedness to Frank Grossklaus of Duesseldorf, Germany, who suggested to me the title for this book and to Thierry Fender of Geneva, Switzerland, who brainstormed with him. I also want to thank these brothers for coining the term "Doctrianity."

Printed in the United States of America.

Contents

1

"Doctrianity" Versus Christianity

Caspar Zacher* trembled in fear as he was led into the courtroom in chains. He glanced around the room, looking for sympathetic faces, but he saw none. Instead, he spied a number of his enemies—townspeople with whom he had argued. Caspar desperately studied the face of the judge for signs of sympathy, but all he saw was a stern countenance. Caspar was convinced he faced certain death.

The year was 1562. The place was the town of Waiblingen in southwestern Germany. The charge: heresy. The scenario was one that had been witnessed countless times in Europe for a thousand years or more. Most of those heresy trials had been conducted by Roman Catholic authorities. However, the authorities whom Caspar faced were Lutheran. Times had changed, but the nature of Christendom had not.

---

*The account of Caspar Zacher's trial was recorded by the bailiff of Waiblingen in an official letter to Duke Christoph, dated July 12, 1562.

Caspar could scarcely keep from trembling when his turn came to stand before the judge. The charges were read. He was being accused of heresy—specifically of belonging to a group known as the Anabaptists. When asked to enter his plea, Caspar emphatically denied the claim.

"I'm a good Lutheran," Caspar protested. "I've never had anything to do with those horrid people!"

The state then methodically presented its case against Caspar. One by one, various townspeople took the stand and testified against him. Several people described Caspar as an envious man, always coveting what others had. Nearly every witness testified that Caspar was extremely quarrelsome, frequently getting into arguments and fights with others. They pointed out that they heard him swear and curse in public many times. A few witnesses reported that he nearly always carried a knife or sword with him when he went out of his house. The whole town hated him.

When the witnesses finished testifying, Caspar was certain he would be found guilty. He knew he couldn't deny the truth of what the witnesses had said. Looking Caspar straight in the eyes, the judge cleared his throat and began to speak:

"Having heard all the evidence presented by the state's witnesses, this court finds the defendant, Caspar Zacher . . ."

Caspar swallowed hard, dreading to hear the judge's next word.

". . . innocent."

Caspar could hardly believe his ears.

The judge went on to explain his decision: "The witnesses are uniform in testifying that you are an envious and quarrelsome man. You frequently curse in public, and you go about town carrying weapons. You are a thoroughly disagreeable man, justly hated by your fellow townsmen. But, fortunately, you are obviously not one of those detestable heretics, the Anabaptists. For the life you live is exactly opposite theirs. They would never have you. You are just as you say, an orthodox Christian."[1]

It was a happy day for Caspar Zacher, but a black day for Christianity. A man was acquitted of heresy because he lived an ungodly life!

What had become of the church Christ founded, so that a holy life was associated with heresy and an ungodly life with orthodoxy? Indeed, a lot had happened to Christ's church—at least, as to the visible body of professing Christians. What happened can be summed up in a nutshell: Christianity had become "Doctrianity."

The Transformation of Christianity

When Christianity was young, the focus was on Jesus Christ and His kingdom—not theology. To be sure, there are foundational doctrines that Christians have always considered essential to the faith. But somehow the things considered essential have grown from a few sentences to a long list of theological tenets, many of which were unknown to the early Christians.

In the beginning, Christians understood that the essence of Christianity was an obedient love-faith relationship with Jesus Christ. This was not just any relationship, but a relationship that produced genuine kingdom fruit. Christianity was a religion primarily of the poor and uneducated. There were no seminaries and no theological schools.

But then something happened: Theologians took over the church. Once the theologians took over, the emphasis soon changed from godly fruit to "orthodox" theology. Before long, living a godly life often made people suspect you were a heretic.

Interestingly, the directive that Jesus gave most often to His followers consisted of just two words. But these two words would turn the world upside down: "follow me." Jesus overturned the theological class of His day and announced a kingdom that would be better understood by intellectual babes than by learned academians.

In contrast, when Christian theologians came to power in the fourth century, the focus changed from "follow me" to "study me." Learned theologians claimed to have special insight and understanding of Scripture. The rest of the church were expected to sit back and accept what the theologians told them the Scriptures really meant. Bearing kingdom fruit was no longer the important thing. The essential thing was to subscribe to the "correct" doctrines.

Theologians Versus the Kingdom

It was primarily the religious authorities who opposed the kingdom of God in Jesus' day, and it has been that way ever since. When I use the term *theologian* in this book, I'm referring to the elite class of scholars and their disciples who have set themselves up as the official interpreters of Scripture. I'm in no way criticizing or condemning Christians who desire to learn all that God has revealed to us about Himself, Jesus Christ, mankind, salvation, life after death, and a whole host of other spiritual subjects. Rather, my criticism is aimed at those elitists who claim for themselves the right to interpret Scripture but deny it to others. It also is aimed at the arrogant academics and ecclesiastical authorities who imagine that they understand the New Testament better than the very Christians who lived close to the time of the apostles.

From the time they came into power, such theologians have warred against the true children of the kingdom. For many centuries these theologians warred against them with fire and sword. Now they fight against the children of the kingdom with words.

However, in many ways, the war of words has been more effective than the war of fire and sword. Many kingdom Christians† are intimidated by today's theological bullies. They've completely adopted the theology of their former persecutors. They're afraid to preach or teach Sunday school without consulting the commentaries, theological

---

† By the phrase, "kingdom Christians," I'm referring to Christians who focus on the lifestyle teachings of Jesus, recognizing that God's kingdom is in no way connected to the kingdoms of this world. Such Christians realize that the kingdom of God is a present reality, and they recognize that the essence of Christianity is an obedient love-faith relationship with Jesus Christ. Although living in this world, kingdom Christians live as citizens of Christ's kingdom.

textbooks, and study Bibles of the theologians—for fear they might say something "wrong."

As a result, the theologians are effectively destroying kingdom Christianity from the inside out. In fact, it wouldn't surprise me if today's kingdom Christians will lose most of Jesus' kingdom teachings within a generation or two.

But it doesn't have to be that way. We kingdom Christians can learn to stand up to today's theological bullies. But to be able to do this effectively, we first need to understand what Christianity looked like in the beginning and how theologians got into power. We also need to understand the means theologians use in our day to muffle the kingdom witness of God's Word.

Once we understand these things, it's not hard to unmask most theologians for the spiritual phonies they often are.

2

The First Theologians

When God set apart the Israelites as His special people, He gave them the Law of Moses, which along with Genesis marked the beginning of the Holy Scriptures. After the death of Moses, God told Joshua, "This Book of the Law shall not depart from your mouth, but you shall meditate in it day and night, that you may observe to do according to all that is written in it" (Josh. 1:8). Although most Israelites would not have had a copy of the Scriptures in their personal possession, one responsibility of the priests and Levites was to read the Scriptures to the people so they would be familiar with them (2 Chron. 17:9).

However, God never told the priests and Levites that it was their responsibility or place to *interpret* the Scriptures. God set up no theological hierarchy to construe the Scriptures for the people, nor did He set up any seminaries or divinity schools to train special teachers or theologians in the "proper meaning" of the Law. Rather, through the centuries, God sent prophets to exhort and warn the Israelites when they were departing from God's ways. But the prophets were not theologians, and God never set the prophets up as a hierarchical class.

Because the Israelites repeatedly failed to listen to the instructions of God, He eventually allowed the Assyrians and Babylonians to remove them from the land of Israel and take them into captivity. Years later, a remnant of Jews returned to the Promised Land from Babylon and rebuilt the temple. The period from the rebuilding of the temple until its destruction in A.D. 70 by the Romans is often referred to as the Second Temple era.

During the Second Temple era, the Jews began establishing synagogues. These were places of assembly where Jews could meet for prayer and reading of the Scriptures. Because the Jews at that time were dispersed throughout much of the Mediterranean world, this enabled them to maintain both their identity and the Law of Moses, even though many of them lived quite a distance from the temple.

During this same period, various religious leaders arose who wanted to make certain that the Jewish nation would never again violate the Law of Moses and go into captivity. Among these leaders were the Sadducees (a priestly group) and the Pharisees (who generally were not priests or Levites). There were also learned men known as scribes.

Although these groups of religious leaders began with good intentions, they evolved from being simple pastors and teachers to becoming an elite hierarchical class above the common people. They went from being the right hand men of God to being God's opponents. They changed from genuine spiritual guides for the Jews to spiritual masters who tyrannized the people. They turned from enlightening the people to keeping them in spiritual ignorance. By the time of Jesus, these religious leaders were being addressed by the title *rabbi,* which literally means "my great one."[1]

This elite class of theologians used two basic methods to bully the common Jews and to give the impression that the theologians alone could properly understand the Scriptures. These two means of control were (1) their linguistic skills—particularly their knowledge of Hebrew—and (2) their status as the official interpreters of the Law.

Using Linguistics to Bully

People with linguistic skills can use their abilities to the glory of God and to the benefit of His people. However, linguists also can use their skills to put themselves on a pedestal above their brothers and sisters. They can use their knowledge as a way to bully others who don't have such learning. That's exactly what the Jewish theologians did.

By the time of Jesus, most Jews couldn't fluently speak and understand biblical Hebrew.* Instead, their everyday language was either Aramaic or Greek, depending on where they lived. Although most people could no longer understand Hebrew, the theologians were opposed to translating the

---

* Some modern-day scholars claim that Hebrew was more widely spoken in Jesus' time than what was once believed. They say this because the recently discovered sectarian writings of the Qumran community were in Hebrew. However, I find their claim unconvincing, for the members of the Qumran sect (who were probably Essenes) were not typical Jews. In many respects, the Qumran sectarians were more Pharisaic than the Pharisees themselves. So it's not surprising that they continued to keep Hebrew as a "holy language."

Scriptures into languages that people could understand. They believed the Scriptures were too sacred to translate into other languages. The Scriptures were written in Hebrew, and they must remain in Hebrew! So the Jewish theologians set up schools to teach future theologians the Hebrew language.

In the Aramaic-speaking synagogues of Palestine, Babylon, and other eastern countries, an appointed reader would read the Scriptures to the people in Hebrew. As the Scriptures were read, a scribe or synagogue leader would explain in Aramaic what the passage meant. These loose Aramaic translations or paraphrases were known as Targums. However, the theologians forbade these Targums to be written down. As a result, none of these Aramaic Targums were written down until after the time of Christ. Yet, even when the Targums were finally put into writing, they weren't widely circulated among the ordinary Jews. They were primarily something for the rabbis to read and study.

So the Aramaic-speaking Jews were almost totally dependent on the Jewish theologians for their knowledge of Scripture. Few ordinary Jews would have dared to challenge the teaching of the scribes and other leaders, for the leaders would always be able to say, "Well the Hebrew in this passage actually means so and so," and the ordinary Jew would be unable to dispute that.

Fortunately, the Greek-speaking Jews fared better—although not because of the theologians. Through the providence of God, in the third century B.C., Ptolemy, the Greek ruler of Egypt, invited learned Jews to come to Egypt and translate the

Hebrew Scriptures into Greek. He did this because he was trying to assemble a library containing the written wisdom of all the civilized people on earth. So through Ptolemy, God opened up a way to get around the theologians and make the Scriptures available in a language that most of the Mediterranean world could understand. The Greek translation of the Old Testament made under the authority of Ptolemy is known as the Septuagint, which means "seventy," because seventy translators worked on the project.

One remarkable thing about the Septuagint is that it wasn't translated into the literary Greek of the classics. Instead, it was translated into *koiné* Greek, the common Greek spoken by everyday people. This was an unheard of thing at the time, but God wanted the Scriptures to be in the actual language the common people spoke—not in the literary language of the elite classes.

Even though the Septuagint freed Hellenic Jews from the language bullies, it didn't help their Aramaic-speaking fellow Jews. And the Jewish theologians had another means to maintain spiritual control over even Greek-speaking Jews: their status as the "official interpreters" of the Law.

The Official Interpreters of Scripture

Many commandments of the Law are not spelled out in detail in the Scriptures. For example, the Law says, "Whoever does any work on the Sabbath shall be put to death" (Ex. 35:2). But God didn't give the Israelites a precise definition of what constituted "work." In fact, He gave only one example of what constitutes work—kindling a fire. Obviously, other activities qualified as work. Any reasonable Israelite would have concluded that if kindling a fire constituted work, then so did plowing a field, harvesting crops, or selling merchandise.

But that still left a huge gray area. What about taking a walk? Writing a letter? Tending to an injured person? Taking a bath? Throwing a rock? Do any of those things constitute "work"? Perhaps all of them do, or perhaps none of them do. Who can say? Well, the theologians declared that *they* could say. They based their authority on the fictitious claim that in addition to the written Law of Moses, an oral Law had been passed down from Moses over the centuries through the theologians. This oral law supposedly filled in the gaps in the written law, and only those who studied in the rabbinical schools knew the oral law.

For instance, what if someone wanted to know if throwing a stone on the Sabbath constituted work? Well, the theologians had the answer:

> He who throws an object up to a distance of four cubits on the ground, has violated the Sabbath. However, if he threw an object within the space of four cubits and it rolled *beyond* four cubits, he has not violated the Sabbath. But if he threw an object beyond four cubits and it rolled *back* into four cubits, he is liable. On the other hand, he who throws an object four cubits into the sea is exempt from violating the Sabbath. However, if the object was thrown into shallow water and a public path goes through the water, he who throws four cubits is liable. But what is the measure of shallow water?

"Shallow" means it is less than ten handbreadths in depth.[2]

So, thanks to the theologians, a Jew could know just how God feels about throwing rocks on the Sabbath! What about writing something on the Sabbath—or just doodling with a pen? Well, the theologians had the answer to this as well:

> He who writes two letters of the alphabet during a single spell of inadvertence is liable for violating the Sabbath. But if he wrote with blood, water, milk, honey, fruit juice, dirt from the street, or with anything which does not leave a lasting mark, he is exempt from a violation. Likewise, if he wrote with the back of his hand, with his foot, mouth, or elbow, he has not violated the Sabbath. If he wrote one letter of the alphabet alongside a letter that had already been written [before the Sabbath], he is exempt.[3]

Well, I could go on and on. Sewing two stitches violates the Sabbath, and so does trimming one's fingernails. Setting a bone violates the Sabbath, and so does killing a flea.

Although these theologians imagined that they were doing the work of God, they were actually working against Him. They were corrupting the thinking of the Jewish people with an evil leaven or yeast. But just what was this leaven of the scribes and Pharisees, the theologians of their day?

3

The Leaven of the Theologians

J esus warned His disciples: "Beware of the leaven of the Pharisees and the Sadducees" (Mt. 16:6). The Pharisees and Sadducees were two leading groups of Jewish theologians. When Jesus used the term "leaven" with regard to these theologians, He was referring to their teaching. However, it wasn't some specific teaching in itself but their *whole approach* to teaching and interpreting the Law. And their approach to Scripture was something evil in the sight of God. Four principal evils characterized their approach to Scripture:

- They missed the big picture of what God was telling mankind.
- They added human teaching to Scripture.
- They also negated some of God's commandments.
- They turned the Scriptures into something that only the elite could properly read and interpret.

Missing the Big Picture

The theologians missed the big picture because they focused on the minutiae of the Law instead of the major things: love, mercy, faith, justice, and forgiveness. Jesus described the theologians perfectly when He denounced them, saying: "Woe to you, scribes and Pharisees, hypocrites! For you pay tithe of mint and anise and cummin, and have neglected the weightier matters of the law: justice and mercy and faith. These you ought to have done, without leaving the others undone. Blind guides, who strain out a gnat and swallow a camel!" (Mt. 23:23,24).

By overanalyzing the Law, the theologians ended up missing the whole purpose and spirit of the Law. If you had asked the scribes and Pharisees what were the two greatest commandments, probably most of them could have given you the correct answer: (1) loving God with all our heart, soul, and mind and (2) loving our neighbor as ourselves. However, it would have been an academic answer, the type of answer that would enable them to get an "A" on an exam. They knew the answer in their heads rather than in their hearts.

Sadly, the minutiae the theologians spent their time interpreting rarely had anything to do with love. They didn't create detailed regulations on what it meant to love one's neighbor or to be merciful to someone. Rather, most of their regulations concerned things such as keeping the Sabbath, assessing damages for wrongdoing, the formalities needed for a valid marriage or divorce, Nazirite vows, tithing, and celebrating the Passover. In short, they imagined that the rituals, ceremonies, and holy days were the most important parts of the Law.

Most of the Jewish theologians were able to correctly identify many of the prophecies in the Old Testament about the coming Messiah. Yet, when the

Messiah finally came, they failed to recognize Him. In fact, they ended up putting Him to death. They had lots of knowledge, but little understanding. They never could see the big picture. Yet, thousands of Jews who had little understanding about the intricacies of the Law had no trouble recognizing Jesus as the Messiah when He did appear.

What Is God Seeking?

One purpose of the Law was to prepare the Jews for the Christ and His kingdom. And what sort of people did God want in preparation for His kingdom? People who had entered into an obedient love-faith relationship with Him and bore the fruits of such a relationship. As Micah put it, "He has shown you, O man, what is good; and what does the Lord require of you but to do justly, to love mercy, and to walk humbly with your God?" (Mi. 6:8).

But the theologians vainly imagined that God was seeking persons who had stuffed their heads with *knowledge* from the Scriptures and Jewish tradition. They invented a path to God that required no godly fruit—just head knowledge and a slavish submission to human traditions. They thought God wanted people who knew better than to throw a stone the wrong distance on the Sabbath. They imagined that they honored God and His Word by refusing to say the Divine name, YHWH (which usually is translated into English as Yahweh or Jehovah). They thought they were respecting God's Word by making regulations and rituals concerning the proper physical handling of it: how much space to leave between each letter when copying the Law, the height and width of the scrolls used, rituals to follow after touching the sacred scrolls, and rules about burying scrolls once they became worn.

But that's not what God was seeking. He was looking for *fruit*—fruit such as mercy and love for one's fellowman. Fruit like support and honor for one's parents. As God told the Israelites, "Execute true justice, show mercy and compassion everyone to his brother. Do not oppress the widow or the fatherless, the alien or the poor. Let none of you plan evil in his heart against his brother" (Zech. 7:9,10). And again: "He who oppresses the poor reproaches his Maker, but he who honors Him has mercy on the needy" (Pr. 14:31).

Adding Human Teaching to Scripture

The New Testament describes the Law as a burden (Ac. 15:28). It was onerous enough without any new commandments added to it. If the scribes and Pharisees had truly grasped the heart and mind of God, they would have realized this. But, as we've seen, they couldn't see the big picture. They imagined that what pleased God was a slavish, meticulous obedience to even imaginary details of the Law. So they added additional laws to what God had given.

Now, there is a difference between making new commandments and merely identifying reasonable applications of existing Biblical commandments. After all, the Old Testament community was responsible for enforcing the Mosaic Law. So it was reasonable for them to make sensible applications concerning the Law. Not working on the Sabbath obviously meant something more than just refraining from kindling a fire (the one application specified by God). A man plowing his field on the Sabbath couldn't claim he was innocent just because God hadn't specifically defined work as including plowing. Applications such as this follow basic common sense.

However, when the theologians included in the definition of work such things as setting a broken bone or flattening a lump in a straw mattress before lying down on it, they were loading senseless, heavy burdens on the backs of the people. They were effectively creating new laws.

But there was a second way by which the theologians created new laws. As I've mentioned, the theologians added to God's laws by claiming that there had been an "oral Law" handed down from Moses through the various generations of scribes through the centuries. And this oral Law supposedly contained additional commandments not found in the written Law. For example, the theologians required various ritual washings that are not found in Scripture (Mt. 15:1,2). But the truth is that there never was such an oral Law. It was simply an invention of the theologians.

Negating God's Commandments

A person would think that because the theologians *added* so many regulations to the Law, at least, they didn't *take away* any of the commandments that the Law actually did contain. But here lies the irony of the theologians' leaven. They not only added to the Law, but they also took away. Jesus Himself pointed this out.

For example, one of the principal commandments of the Law was to honor one's father and mother. The word *honor* in English generally carries no connotation other than to show respect. However, it's obvious from reading the New Testament that the underlying Hebrew (*hadar*) and Greek words (*timaoi*) also carry the sense of providing financial support (Mt. 15:4–6; 1 Ti. 5:3,17,18). In other words, it was a specific commandment of God for the Israelites to support their aged parents.

However, the theologians taught that if a person declared that his assets were "corban," he didn't have to use them to support his parents. Declaring property to be Corban meant declaring that it was dedicated to God. Once it was declared to be Corban, no third party had any claim to it.

Now, it was expected that some of the property declared as Corban would be donated to the scribes and Pharisees or to the synagogues they controlled. So this whole system of declaring property to be Corban benefited the Jewish theologians. It also made things convenient for grown children who didn't want any obligation to support their parents. However, this selfish practice contradicted God's express commandment to provide for one's parents, and it left many of the elderly Jews destitute.

Taking the Scriptures From the People

Although the Old Testament was copied and preserved under the supervision of the Jewish religious leaders, the scribal system effectively took the Scriptures away from the people. Because of the teachings of these leaders, the ordinary Jew came to view the inspired Scriptures as inadequate.

After all, would a normal person reading Exodus 35:2—"whoever does any work on the Sabbath shall be put to death"—come to the conclusion that he couldn't swat a flea biting him or that he couldn't scribble his name on a piece of paper? Of course not. Yet, according to the theologians, he was violating the Sabbath, a sin punishable by death. So the Jewish people were afraid to simply listen to the Law and follow a reasonable application of it. To avoid offending God, the community thought they had better let their theologians tell them what the Law really meant.

God had inspired the Scriptures to be written for the common people. But the theologians turned them into something for the spiritual elite, for men trained in the rabbinical schools.

The Total Effect of the Leaven

The sum total of the scribes and Pharisees' human commandments, commentary, interpretations, hypocrisy, and spiritual elitism constituted the leaven Jesus told us to beware of. The weight of the theologians' leaven crushed the whole spirit and purpose of the Law. The Scriptures in themselves became useless, because they only meant whatever the theologians said they meant.

There was no point for an individual to try studying the sacred writings on his own. The average Jew felt that he or she couldn't possibly understand the Scriptures without the aid of the theologians. For in the end, the Jewish theologians had made the Scriptures invalid because of their traditions. The theologians controlled what the people learned about God and His dealings with man. Yet, they were themselves in utter darkness.

To me, the situation was similar to an ancient sailing ship. When a new ship left port, it could move with considerable speed. However, barnacles soon began attaching themselves to the hull of the ship. Over the years, more and more barnacles attached themselves to the hull, weighing down the ship. Eventually, the weight of the barnacles slowed the ship to a crawl. At that point, the ship had to be put into dry dock and the barnacles removed. Otherwise, the ship was practically useless.

The leaven of the scribes and Pharisees had done the same thing to Scripture. God had given the Israelites the exact inspired writings they needed. But over the years, these Jewish theologians had added so much of their leaven to the Scriptures that they became like a ship weighed down with barnacles. It was time for someone to clean off the barnacles!

4

How Jesus Overturned the Theologians

When Jesus entered the scene, He wasted no time scraping off the barnacles. In fact, before Jesus even began His ministry, the Spirit had sent out John the Baptist to prepare the way. And John launched the opening salvo against the Jewish theologians by talking about their *fruit*. He said to them: "Brood of vipers! Who warned you to flee from the wrath to come? Therefore bear fruits worthy of repentance, and do not think to say to yourselves, 'We have Abraham as our father.' For I say to you that God is able to raise up children to Abraham from these stones" (Mt. 3:7–9).

We've already seen why the Jewish theologians deserved to be denounced in such strong terms. They had tried to create a way to God that didn't require godly fruit. As Jesus explained it: "Woe to you lawyers! For you have taken away the key of knowledge. You did not enter in yourselves, and those who were entering in you hindered" (Lk. 11:52). The lawyers Jesus denounced were not attorneys. In fact, Jewish society in Jesus' day had no such thing as attorneys. The lawyers of which He spoke were the theologians—the so-called experts in the Law.

They saw themselves as the protectors and defenders of the Law. But in reality, they were just the opposite. They had corrupted the Law and had taken away "the key of knowledge" from the common people. The theologians had made the people totally dependent on them for access to the Scriptures and to the knowledge of God. But then they blocked the way to the kingdom. They produced no kingdom fruit themselves, and they hindered others from producing fruit as well.

In the course of His ministry, Jesus destroyed the two methods by which the theologians had held the people in bondage. As we've seen, one of those methods was their superior knowledge of the Hebrew language. Did Jesus endorse Hebrew as a holy language, the only language suitable for God's messages to mankind? Not at all. Instead, the only record we have of His teachings is in *Greek*.*

Jesus totally bypassed Hebrew. Unlike the theologians, He didn't train His disciples to read Hebrew so they could read Scripture in its "original language." In fact, when Jesus' apostles quoted from the Old Testament, they nearly always quoted from the Greek Septuagint, not from the Hebrew versions used by the theologians.

Similarly, rather than recognizing the scribes and Pharisees as the "official interpreters of the Law," Jesus called them "blind guides" who had missed the whole point of the Law. The theologians were con-

---

* By this, I don't mean that Jesus necessarily taught in Greek. (Most linguists assume that he taught in Aramaic.) Yet, through the New Testament, His teachings were given to the world in Greek—not Hebrew or Aramaic.

stantly perturbed at Jesus because He contradicted their teachings.

Unmasking the Theologians

As we've discussed, Jesus labeled the whole Jewish theological system as leaven of which the children of the kingdom needed to beware. Because of their finicky interpretations of the Law, Jesus denounced the religious leaders for binding heavy burdens on the people that were "hard to bear" (Mt. 23:4).

Furthermore, Jesus rejected their claims to be preserving the oral traditions handed down from Moses. Instead, He deliberately ignored their traditions, because they were man-made. For example, notice what happened when He accepted an invitation to dine with a Pharisee:

> As He spoke, a certain Pharisee asked Him to dine with him. So He went in and sat down to eat. When the Pharisee saw *it,* he marveled that He had not first washed before dinner. Then the Lord said to him, "Now you Pharisees make the outside of the cup and dish clean, but your inward part is full of greed and wickedness. Foolish ones! Did not He who made the outside make the inside also? But rather give alms of such things as you have; then indeed all things are clean to you" (Lk. 11:37–41).

On another occasion Jesus addressed the same issue about the ceremonial washings of the theologians: "Laying aside the commandment of God, you hold the tradition of men—the washing of pitchers and cups, and many other such things you do" (Mk. 7:8). All of the theologians' extrabiblical commandments were not really the oral law passed down from Moses. They were just the traditions of men.

Not only that, Jesus called the theologians to task in the strongest language for nullifying God's commandments. He told them, "[You are] making the word of God of no effect through your tradition which you have handed down. And many such things you do" (Mk. 7:13).

No Theologians in the Kingdom

However, Jesus went much further than simply denouncing the scribes and Pharisees as hypocrites and attacking their teachings. The problem wasn't merely that *these* particular theologians were teaching the wrong things. The problem was the very existence of a theological class. That's because theologians will inevitably end up corrupting God's message. They will always place head knowledge above fruit. If God had wanted a class of theologians, He would have set one up in the first place. God doesn't need theologians as the official interpreters of Scripture. His Word is sufficient. For that reason, Jesus told His disciples the following about the scribes and Pharisees:

> They love the best places at feasts, the best seats in the synagogues, greetings in the marketplaces, and to be called by men, "Rabbi, Rabbi." But you, do not be called "Rabbi;"for One is your Teacher, the Christ, and you are all brethren. Do not call anyone on earth your father; for One is your Father, He who is in heaven. And do not be called teachers; for One is your Teacher, the Christ. But he who is greatest among you shall be your servant. And whoever exalts himself will be humbled, and he who humbles himself will be exalted (Mt. 23:6–12).

One of the problems with the whole theological system is that it sets up certain men as superior to others. What's more, theologians end up invalidating much of God's Word—no matter how well-intentioned they may be. The kingdom of God needs simple pastors and teachers, but not theologians above their ordinary brothers.

Throughout His ministry, Jesus made it clear that His kingdom needed no theological class. To enter the kingdom, a person doesn't need to sit at the feet of some learned theologian. It's just the opposite. He needs to humble himself and become as a little child.

"At that time the disciples came to Jesus, saying, 'Who then is greatest in the kingdom of heaven?' Then Jesus called a little child to Him, set him in the midst of them, and said, 'Assuredly, I say to you, unless you are converted and become as little children, you will by no means enter the kingdom of heaven. Therefore whoever humbles himself as this little child is the greatest in the kingdom of heaven. Whoever receives one little child like this in My name receives Me'" (Mt. 18:1–5).

In fact, in the kingdom, not only is special theological training not necessary—it's actually a hindrance. Intellectual "babes" can understand matters of the kingdom better than cerebral academics. As Jesus said, "I thank You, Father, Lord of heaven and earth, that You have hidden these things from the wise and prudent and have revealed them to babes" (Mt. 11:25). By "wise and prudent," Jesus is obviously referring to the worldly wise and prudent. Other translators have rendered this phrase: "the learned and the clever" or "the wise and learned."[1]

Theological schooling is of no help in matters pertaining to the kingdom. If anything, it's a hindrance.

When Jesus preached about "babes" entering the kingdom, He wasn't voicing some empty slogan that He Himself didn't follow. No, He chose as His twelve apostles men who had no theological training. In fact, many of them had little schooling. They were ordinary, unlettered men. The training He gave them was hands-on experience. Jesus didn't set up any seminaries, theological schools or academies as did the scribes and Greek philosophers. Rather, He had his disciples accompany Him on His preaching missions, and He later sent them out on missions of their own to obtain experience (Mt. 10). He made *disciples*, not academics.

The Kingdom in Operation

Nothing changed in this basic system after Jesus ascended to heaven. The fishermen and ordinary people whom Jesus had placed in positions of leadership proved themselves quite capable of the task. People flocked into the kingdom, and the spiritual shepherds were able to give them good teaching and care. In fact, the kingdom followers of Jesus grew rapidly. Seeing this, the Jewish theologians realized they would either have to stop it—or else eventually lose their own positions of power. So they had their soldiers arrest Peter and John—the two former fishermen among the leaders of this new movement. The Jewish theologians were quite certain they would be able to intimidate these "ignorant fishermen" into keeping quiet.

However, that's not how things worked out. Rather than being cowed by the theologians, as were most Jews, Peter answered them fearlessly. The Jewish theologians had wanted to know by what power he and John had healed a man. Filled with the Holy Spirit, Peter boldly replied, "Let it be known to you all, and to all the people of Israel, that by the name of Jesus Christ of Nazareth, whom you crucified, whom God raised from the dead, by Him this man stands here before you whole" (Acts 4:10).

The religious leaders were taken aback: "Now when they saw the boldness of Peter and John, and perceived that they were uneducated and untrained men, they marveled. And they realized that they had been with Jesus. And seeing the man who had been healed standing with them, they could say nothing against it" (Acts 4:13). So they decided to let Peter and John go, but with a stern warning to speak no more about Jesus.

But the days when the theologians held a spiritual power monopoly in Judea were over. Peter and John responded to the theologians' threat with the bold declaration: "Whether it is right in the sight of God to listen to you more than to God, you judge. For we cannot but speak the things which we have seen and heard" (Acts. 4:19,20).

As the years passed, nothing changed. It was still the ordinary and uneducated men who led the church. The apostles neither set up any seminaries nor provided any other theological schooling for the next generation of leaders. Paul described how things worked in the kingdom of God:

Christ did not send me to baptize, but to preach the gospel, not with wisdom of words, lest the cross of Christ should be made of no effect. For the message of the cross is foolishness to those who are perishing, but to us who are being saved it is the power of God. For it is written: "I will destroy the wisdom of the wise, And bring to nothing the understanding of the prudent." Where is the wise? Where is the scribe? Where is the disputer of this age? Has not God made foolish the wisdom of this world? . . .

Because the foolishness of God is wiser than men, and the weakness of God is stronger than men. For you see your calling, brethren, that not many wise according to the flesh, not many mighty, not many noble, are called. But God has chosen the foolish things of the world to put to shame the wise" (1 Cor. 1:17–28).

5

The Kingdom of Children

However, someone may object, saying that Paul himself had been trained in the rabbinical schools. That is correct. The door to the kingdom is not barred to those who have an advanced education. God is able to use such people in His kingdom—but only if they're willing to humble themselves and come into the kingdom as a little child. To serve Christ, Paul had to largely discard most of his rabbinical training.

In fact, Paul told the Corinthians, "And I, brethren, when I came to you, did not come with excellence of speech or of wisdom declaring to you the testimony of God. For I determined not to know anything among you except Jesus Christ and Him crucified. I was with you in weakness, in fear, and in much trembling. And my speech and my preaching were not with persuasive words of human wisdom, but in demonstration of the Spirit and of power, that your faith should not be in the wisdom of men but in the power of God" (1 Cor. 2:1–5).

Unpolished Language of Scripture

The unbelieving Gentiles gave testimony to the truth of what Paul said. He did not write with "persuasive words of human wisdom" or with "excellence of speech." In the second century, when Christian writings made their way into the hands of the Romans, the Romans laughed at the humble diction used by Paul and the other New Testament writers. In fact, when I first read the disparaging things the unbelieving Romans said about the New Testament writings, I was surprised.

Now, I had known ever since I was a teenager that the New Testament had been written in *koiné* Greek, common Greek—not classical Greek. But I thought this was something more akin to American English versus British English. I didn't realize that to the ears of educated Gentiles, *koiné* Greek was simply poor diction, something unsuitable for serious literature.

The early Christians never denied the fact that the New Testament was written in unpolished Greek. In his *Apology,* Justin Martyr told the Romans, "Renouncing the error of your fathers, you should read the prophecies of the sacred writers, not expecting to find in them polished diction."[1] One of Justin Martyr's converts, a man named Tatian, frankly admitted: "I was led to put faith in the Scriptures by the unpretentious nature of the language."[2]

Origen defended the unpolished language of Scripture against some of Christianity's severest and ablest critics. He explained to them, "Our prophets, the apostles, and Jesus Himself were careful to adopt a style of speech that would not only convey the truth, but that would be suitable to gain over the multitude. . . . For, if I may venture to say so, few have benefited from the beautiful and polished style of Plato and others who have written like him. . . . It is easy, indeed, to observe that Plato is found only in the hands of those who profess to be literary men."[3] And again, "We are not to imagine that a truth adorned with the graces of Grecian speech is necessarily better than the same when expressed in the more humble and unpretentious language used by Jews [i.e., the Septuagint] and Christians."[4]

Origen writes further: "See, then, if Plato and the wise men among the Greeks, in the beautiful things they say, are not like those physicians who confine their attentions to what are called the 'better classes of society,' and who despise the multitudes. In contrast, the prophets among the Jews and the disciples of Jesus scorn mere elegances of style and what is called in Scripture, 'the wisdom according to the flesh.' . . . They resemble those who investigate to provide the most wholesome food for the largest number of persons. For this purpose, they adapt their language and style to the capacities of the common people."[5]

The early Christian apologist Arnobius answered the Romans: "[You say] our Scriptures were written by unlearned and ignorant men and that, therefore, they should not be readily believed. But is this not actually a *stronger* reason to believe? For our writings have not been adulterated by any false statements. Rather, they were produced by men of simple minds, who did not know how to make their accounts deceitful with flashy language. For truth never seeks deceitful polish. . . . You accuse our writings of having disgraceful blemishes. However, do not your most perfect and wonderful books contain these grammatical errors as well?"[6]

When you hear Arnobius acknowledge that there are grammatical "errors" in the New Testament, you shouldn't think this is in conflict with a belief in the inerrancy of Scripture. He simply means that the New Testament writers—including Paul—broke some of the rules of conventional literary Greek grammar, for they were writing for the common people who knew nothing of such "rules." But, once again, his words are a powerful witness that in the first century, Christians came mainly from the uneducated classes. And the Holy Spirit saw fit to inspire the New Testament Scriptures to be written in the language of the common people, the uneducated masses, rather than in polished literary Greek. It all followed the pattern that Jesus had laid out.

Language Study?

Not only did the apostles open up the New Testament to everyday men and women by writing in common *koiné* Greek, but they also liberated the Old Testament. As we've discussed, the Jewish theologians had imprisoned God's Word in Hebrew, a language that even most Jews could no longer speak—let alone the Gentiles. Instead of following the example of these theologians, the apostles ignored the Hebrew scrolls of the scribes and adopted the Greek Septuagint instead. As I've mentioned, when they quote the Old Testament in their writings, they nearly always do so out of the Greek Septuagint. In fact, the Septuagint became *the* Old Testament for Christians everywhere. In the first century, Greek was the international language of the west and much of the Mideast. It was spoken by Romans, Greeks, and western Jews alike. By adopting the Septuagint, Jesus' disciples opened up all of the Scriptures—both Old and New—to the world at large.

In contrast to both the Jewish theologians and modern day Christian theologians, the apostles and their disciples set up no schools to train men in language studies. They never encouraged anyone to learn Hebrew or Aramaic so they could read the Old Testament in the "original languages." Likewise, when the first Christians preached in parts of the world that didn't speak Greek, they didn't train men to study Greek so that they could read the New Testament in its original language. Instead, bilingual Christians quickly translated both the Septuagint and the New Testament into widely read languages such as Latin and Syriac (the predominant dialect of Aramaic at that time).

Simple Theology

There was a reason why the first-century Christians weren't meticulous in their use of Greek, nor concerned with training others to read Greek or Hebrew. It was that Christianity originally centered on Christ and His kingdom—not on fine points of theology. It's rather difficult to put together a detailed theological statement just from the teachings of Jesus. That's because in essence the gospel of the kingdom is not theology. It's about people entering into an obedient love-faith relationship with Jesus, the King, and bearing fruit. Jesus didn't talk much about theology because that wasn't particularly important to Him. However, He did talk a lot about fruit. And He talked a lot about how we are to live as citizens of His kingdom. He taught us what it means to love one another and to love God. Those things *are* important to Him.

6

But Wasn't Paul a Theologian?

You may be thinking to yourself, "But that can't be true. Look at Paul. Surely he was a theologian." In fact, secularists and liberal theologians often claim that Paul was the real architect of Christianity. They imagine this because what passes as Biblical Christianity today in most churches stems primarily from Martin Luther's interpretation of Paul's writings. Luther's gospel was not based on Jesus' teachings, but on a misconstrued understanding of Paul's writings. But if we must focus on Paul's letters to establish the Christian faith, then truly the servant has become greater than his Master.

The reason most of us read Paul's letters as though they are doctrinal treatises is because that's how they've been presented to us all of our lives. In the chapters to come, we'll be looking at the Christian theologians over the centuries who hijacked Christianity. As learned theologians, they read their own concept of Christianity back into the Scriptures. Because they imagined that theology is the essence of Christianity, they turned Paul into a theologian like themselves. In fact, they made him the ultimate Christian theologian.

It's similar to what's happened with the teaching of evolution. Few people from their own unbiased observation would imagine that the complex biological systems on earth got here simply through blind accident. Nobody would look at a beautiful horse and imagine that it had evolved over millions of years from a single-cell organism.

However, most non-Christians think in those terms today because everything they read about plants or animals always states that these things evolved over millions of years. The theory of evolution dominates every textbook, every encyclopedia, and virtually every book and magazine article produced by the secular world. Consequently, most people today "see" evolution in everything around them because they've been programmed to see things that way.

A similar thing is true in Christianity. The theologians have dominated Christian thinking and writing for so long that the typical Christian today reads the Scriptures through the eyes of these theologians. So Paul becomes the great theologian. Even the writings of the "ordinary and uneducated" fisherman, the apostle John, become theological treatises.

I know that I've read the New Testament writings through such theological glasses for most of my life. Yet, even when I was overly focused on theology, a question always nagged me: If the New Testament epistles are so focused on theology, why aren't Jesus' teachings? Why does *He* primarily talk about the kingdom and living the kingdom life—and so little about theological doctrines? And how can it be true that God has "hidden these things from the wise and prudent" and has "revealed them to babes" if men have to train in seminaries and become "wise and prudent" to properly understand the Scriptures? Somehow all this never added up.

But Don't the Scriptures Talk About Doctrine?

However, you may reply, "But the New Testament has a lot to say on the subject of *doctrine*. For example, Jesus said about the scribes and Pharisees: 'In vain they worship Me, teaching as doctrines the commandments of men.'" (Mt. 15:9). And that's true. When the church first got started, Acts tells us that the new believers "continued steadfastly in the apostles' *doctrine* and fellowship, in the breaking of bread, and in prayers" (Ac. 2:42). Furthermore, Paul said that "we should no longer be children, tossed to and fro and carried about with every wind of *doctrine*, by the trickery of men, in the cunning craftiness of deceitful plotting" (Eph. 4:14). Finally, the Epistle to the Hebrews warns us "not be carried about with various and strange *doctrines*" (Heb. 13:9).

Paul particularly talks a lot about doctrine in his pastoral epistles. He told Timothy, "Now the Spirit expressly says that in latter times some will depart from the faith, giving heed to deceiving spirits and *doctrines* of demons" (1 Ti. 4:1). He told him, "All Scripture is given by inspiration of God, and is profitable for *doctrine*, for reproof, for correction, for instruction in righteousness" (2 Ti. 3:16). He warned Timothy that "the time will come when they will not endure sound *doctrine*" (2 Ti. 4:3). And Paul told Titus that one of the qualifications for an elder is that he is "holding fast the faithful word as he has been taught" so that "he may be able, by sound *doctrine*, both to exhort and convict those who contradict" (Tit. 1:9).

So you may be saying to yourself, "Well, David, doctrine *is* important after all." And I agree. But what is doctrine?

What Is Doctrine?

When most Christians hear the word *doctrine,* they think of theological teachings or dogma. That is how the word is used almost exclusively today in Christian circles. But originally the English word "doctrine" simply meant teaching, just as the word "doctor" originally meant teacher. That's how people understood those words in the days of William Tyndale and King James I. However, in the intervening centuries, doctrine has primarily come to mean theological dogma.

So when Christians read that term in the New Testament today, they come away with an entirely different meaning than did Christians in the days of King James. They also come away with a different meaning than did the first-century Christians. That's because the Greek words translated in our Bibles as "doctrine"—*didache* and *didaskalia*—simply mean teaching or instruction. They have no connotation of "theological dogma."

Actually, the original meaning of "doctrine" becomes clear from the context of many Scripture passages that use the term. When Paul wrote Timothy about doctrine, he was primarily referring to teachings that affect the Christian life. For example, he said: "We know that the Law is good if one uses it lawfully, knowing this: that the Law is not made for a righteous person, but for the lawless and insubordinate, for the ungodly and for sinners, for the unholy and profane, for murderers of fathers and murderers of mothers, for manslayers, for fornicators, for sodomites, for kidnappers, for liars, for perjurers, and if there is any other thing that is contrary to sound *doctrine*" (1 Ti.1:8–10). So people who murder, lie, and live immorally are living contrary to sound doctrine.

Again, Paul wrote Timothy: "If you instruct the brethren in these things, you will be a good minister of Jesus Christ, nourished in the words of faith and of the good doctrine which you have carefully followed" (1 Ti. 4:6). So doctrine is not just something you believe, but something you follow.

For example, being disobedient to believing masters was a product of false doctrine: "Those who have believing masters, let them not despise them because they are brethren, but rather serve them because those who are benefited are believers and beloved. Teach and exhort these things. If anyone teaches otherwise and does not consent to wholesome words, even the words of our Lord Jesus Christ, and to the doctrine which accords with godliness, he is proud, knowing nothing" (1 Ti. 6:2–4).

In one of His final exhortations to Christians, Jesus rebuked the church at Pergamum for holding to the "doctrine of Balaam." Was the doctrine of Balaam some theological system? Not at all. Jesus explains, "But I have a few things against you, because you have there those who hold the doctrine of Balaam, who taught Balak to put a stumbling block before the children of Israel, to eat things sacrificed to idols, and to commit sexual immorality" (Rev. 2:14). So the "doctrine of Balaam" encouraged idolatry and sexual immorality.

You may be asking yourself, "Can doctrine ever refer to theological teaching as well? Yes, it is occasionally used that way in Scripture. After all, because doctrine means "teaching," it encompasses theological teaching as well as lifestyle teaching. For example, the writer of Hebrews uses it in that sense when he writes: "Therefore, leaving the discussion of the elementary principles of Christ, let us go on to perfection, not laying again the foundation of repentance from dead works and of faith toward God, of the doctrine of baptisms, of laying on of hands, of resurrection of the dead, and of eternal judgment" (Heb. 6:1,2).

Here the writer talks about fundamental theological teachings and uses the word *doctrine*. However, did you notice how extremely simple these elementary theological doctrines of Christianity are? He mentions only five or six basic things—and these can be summed up in one sentence. Furthermore, even an unlearned person who reads the New Testament would have no trouble seeing those basic teachings.

Similarly, John uses *doctrine* in the sense of theological beliefs in his Second Epistle, where he writes: "For many deceivers have gone out into the world who do not confess Jesus Christ as coming in the flesh. This is a deceiver and an antichrist. Look to yourselves, that we do not lose those things we worked for, but that we may receive a full reward. Whoever transgresses and does not abide in the doctrine of Christ does not have God. He who abides in the doctrine of Christ has both the Father and the Son. If anyone comes to you and does not bring this doctrine, do not receive him into your house nor greet him; for he who greets him shares in his evil deeds" (2 Jn. 1:7–11).

Two things from this passage are particularly noteworthy. First, the doctrine mentioned is an extremely basic theological belief. Anyone who doesn't believe that Jesus came in the flesh simply doesn't accept the New Testament as true. The group to whom John was referring were the Gnostics. They rejected all the Old Testament and so much of the teachings of Jesus and His apostles that they essentially created an entirely new religion. But it wasn't only their theology that John was concerned with. Because they said that nothing in the material world matters, most Gnostic groups taught it was perfectly acceptable to live an immoral and licentious life. So John was just as concerned about their "evil deeds" as he was about their twisted theology.

Jesus Never Changes

Jesus drove one final nail in the coffin of the theologians. And that final nail was this: He never changes. "Jesus Christ is the same yesterday, today, and forever" (Heb. 13:8). Jesus is always the one Teacher, the one Scribe, because His teachings are final. His teachings didn't need to be reinterpreted in the second century, or the twelfth century, or the eighteenth century. Nor do they need to be reinterpreted in the twenty-first century. Whatever Jesus' words meant to His original hearers is exactly what they mean today.

That's because Jesus' teachings are not mere human teaching like the U.S. Constitution. For a man-made instrument, the Constitution is a remarkable document. But parts of it get reinterpreted just about every year—whether that was the intent of the Founding Fathers or not. Nowadays, the Constitution has essentially been replaced by the Supreme Court as the final source of legal authority in the United States. Anymore, the Constitution means whatever the Supreme Court says it means. The nine justices of the Supreme Court are the theological class of the American legal world.

But it's not that way with the gospel. Jesus didn't set up an ongoing institution of theologians to reinterpret His teachings to each new generation. He didn't need to revise His teachings so they would still be fresh and "relevant" in each succeeding generation. Only man-made teachings need such revision. The gospel of the kingdom never needs updating. It's always fresh, and it's always relevant to each new generation. People who think they need to make the gospel "relevant" by changing it are reducing Jesus to a mere human teacher whose teachings quickly get outdated.

In short, the kingdom worked out exactly as Jesus said it would. The people whom the world looks down upon as foolish and ignorant are the very ones who have best understood the kingdom of God. And the people whom the world looks up to as brilliant generally have been the ones who have had the hardest time grasping the simple truths that Jesus and His disciples taught.

7

The Next Generation After the Apostles

The apostles didn't appoint a second group of twelve apostles to replace themselves after they died. In fact, the apostles themselves didn't serve as a rabbinical body, a second Sanhedrin. After the Ascension, they remained together in Jerusalem only for a few years. After that, they all went their separate ways, taking the kingdom gospel throughout the world.[1] There is no indication that there were any further meetings of the apostles after the one described in the fifteenth chapter of Acts.

So how did the apostles prepare the next generation of leaders in the church? Did they write theological works for men in leadership to study? No, kingdom training worked exactly the same way it had when Jesus was on earth. The apostles gave hands-on training to other men such as Mark, Titus, and Timothy. The next generation of leaders learned by working alongside more experienced leaders. As Paul told Timothy, "The things that you have heard from me among many witnesses, commit these to faithful men who will be able to teach others also" (2 Ti. 2:2).

And that's the reason the simple message of the kingdom gospel continued on after the apostles died. They had committed it to "faithful men" who were able to teach the next generation. The apostles did such a superb job that the second-century church was able to overcome both the Gnostic heretics who tried to hijack the church and the fierce persecution the pagan Romans leveled against Christians. And the second-century Christians did this without establishing a new theological class or losing sight of the kingdom.

As it was in the days of the apostles, there were no seminaries or other schools to train church leaders in the second century. In fact, there weren't even any systematic theologians in that period. Men were appointed as elders and bishops because they met the spiritual qualifications set forth in the New Testament—not because they were educated men or because they had a diploma from a seminary. Their only training came from serving under spiritual leaders in the local church.

It was mainly the uneducated and poor—the intellectual infants—who comprised the bulk of the church. To be sure, there *were* well-educated Christians in the second century, but most of them had obtained their education before they had ever heard of Christ. After they surrendered their lives to Jesus, some of these men put their education to good use by defending Christianity with their pens. Justin Martyr, Mark Felix, and Athenagoras are examples of men who used their learning in the service of the kingdom. But these men held no office in the church, and they didn't wield any ecclesiastical power. They were in no sense theologians. Nor were they "church fathers," as they are often mistakenly called. They simply were kingdom soldiers who made good use of the abilities and learning they had.

The Historic Faith
Centered on Jesus' Teachings

Christians in the second century remained children of the kingdom. They continued to recognize that the teachings of Jesus—not Paul*—were the central tenets of Christianity. When they wanted to explain to non-believers what Christianity was all about, the second-century Christians went straight to the teachings of Jesus. For example, the oldest Christian apology (i.e., defense of Christianity) that still exists in its entirety is the *First Apology* of Justin Martyr. In it, Justin Martyr explains to the Roman officials what Christianity is all about and what Christians believe. He tells them:

> The *teachings of Jesus* have transformed our lives. We who previously delighted in immorality now

---

* In reality, there is no contradiction between Paul and Jesus. However, theologians have misconstrued Paul's writings to subvert the clear teachings of Christ. Like his Master, Paul taught that we cannot inherit eternal life without godly fruit. He wrote, "Now the works of the flesh are evident, which are: adultery, fornication, uncleanness, lewdness, idolatry, sorcery, hatred, contentions, jealousies, outbursts of wrath, selfish ambitions, dissensions, heresies [i.e., divisions], envy, murders, drunkenness, revelries, and the like; of which I tell you beforehand, just as I also told you in time past, that those who practice such things will not inherit the kingdom of God. But the fruit of the Spirit is love, joy, peace, longsuffering, kindness, goodness, faithfulness, gentleness, self-control" (Gal. 5:19–23).

embrace chastity exclusively. We who used to practice magical arts now devote our lives to the Good and Unbegotten God. We who valued the acquisition of wealth and possessions above all things now bring what we have into a common pool and share with everyone in need.

Many of us used to hate and destroy one another. We wouldn't live with people of a different race because of their different customs. But now, since the coming of Christ, we live familiarly with such people, and we pray for our enemies. We seek to persuade those who unjustly hate us to live by the wonderful teachings of Christ so that they can enjoy the wonderful hope of God's reward with us. . . .

The teachings of Christ were brief and concise. He was not skilled in devious argumentation, but rather His word was the power of God."[2]

Justin Martyr then proceeds to set forth the teachings of Jesus, quoting almost exclusively from the Sermon on the Mount. If you had asked any of the early Christians what the heart of the gospel was, they all would have answered, "the Sermon on the Mount." Christianity centered on the fruit that comes from an obedient love-faith relationship with Jesus, with a focus on His teachings from the Sermon on the Mount.

Fruit Versus Theology

The second-century Christians stood in a blessed position. They were the last generation of Christians who could personally know what had been handed down from the apostolic age. When they talked about the historic faith, they spoke of what they had personally heard from the apostles or from the "faithful men" whom the apostles had trained.

Logically, we might expect to find that the theology in the early second century was far more complex than the theology we have today—because it was so close to the time of the apostles. However, the truth is just the opposite. All the theology the second-century Christians considered essential could be summed up in a few sentences.

Several writers from the second century bear witness to the simple statement of theology to which the early Christians universally subscribed. One of these was Tertullian, who wrote: "The rule of faith, indeed, is altogether one, alone immoveable and unchangeable. The rule is:

> To believe in only one God Almighty, the Creator of the universe, and His Son Jesus Christ, born of the virgin Mary, crucified under Pontius Pilate, raised again the third day from the dead, received in the heavens, sitting now at the right hand of the Father, destined to come to judge the living and the dead through the resurrection of the flesh."[3]

That uncomplicated statement of belief contains only 63 words. To give you an indication of just how much Christianity has changed since its early years, the Westminster Confession of Faith promulgated by the Puritans in the seventeenth century contains 12,079 words. In fact, one of the things I've noticed in studying church history is the further a person gets from the time of Christ, the more theological dogma there is. The "essentials of the faith" somehow kept growing through the centuries. But how can that be?

The apostles and disciples had recognized that the faith was already complete in *their* day. Before A.D. 60, Paul could boldly declare, "If anyone preaches any other gospel to you than what you have received, let him be accursed" (Ga. 1:9). Jude exhorted Christians to "contend earnestly for the faith which was once for all delivered to the saints" (Jude 3). So there would be no more theologians and no further definitions of the Christian faith after the apostles.

Jesus wasn't ever going to change, and there would be no further master teachers after Him. The second-century Christians recognized the finality of the gospel. They didn't add man-made dogma to what they had received. They had received a simple faith, and they kept it that way. Their focus was on the Christ-life, not theology.

Now please don't misunderstand me. The early Christians had theological beliefs about most of the same matters that our doctrinal statements cover. And their beliefs nearly always followed a literal understanding of Scripture on every subject. However, they never felt that a person had to understand most of those things correctly to be a true Christian. They never elevated such teachings to being essentials of the faith or something to build a church upon.

Because the faith received from the apostles was so simple, we should question any new dogmas that go beyond that simple faith. If a continuity of belief can't be traced back to A.D. 100, we can hardly claim that it's the historic faith.

A God Who Doesn't Specialize in Theology

As I've said, second-century Christianity was truly a religion of the "ordinary and unlearned." A Christian in that age could read and innocently talk about what he understood the Scriptures to be saying without fear of being hauled before the theological police for saying something he shouldn't have said.

The way the second-century children of the kingdom perceived God is aptly reflected in the words of the sixteenth century writer and early Christian scholar, Richard Hooker. He said, "God is no nitpicking sophist, eager to trip us up whenever we say something amiss, but a courteous tutor, ready to amend what, in our weakness or our ignorance, we say in error, and to make the most of what we say correctly."[4]

To the ears of many, this may sound very liberal. But the early Christians weren't liberal; they were *conservative*. The apostles hadn't built up complicated theological systems, so the early Christians weren't going to do so either. The apostles hadn't written any theological tomes, so the second-century Christians didn't write any either. If the original gospel was simple enough for the uneducated to understand, so was the gospel in the second century.

If someone innocently misunderstood a statement made by Jesus or His apostles, the second-century church simply brushed it off. They figured that God would overlook what we may misunderstand in our human ignorance. The early Christians served a God whose grace and mercy cover unintentional theological errors.

To be sure, there were theological boundaries in the early church, but the simple statement of belief we read earlier pretty well marked where those boundaries lay. The groups excluded by the early Christians, such as the Gnostics, went beyond those rather simple boundaries.

What Is Heresy?

Today, the word "heresy" has come to mean an opinion at variance with "orthodox" theology. But that's not at all what the Greek word *hairesis* meant in New Testament times. It meant a faction or party, such as in Acts 5:17, where it speaks of the "sect (*hairesis*) of the Sadducees." It's the same word Paul used in writing the Corinthians: "When you come together as a church, I hear that there are divisions among you, and in part I believe it. For there must also be factions (*hairesis*) among you, that those who are approved may be recognized among you" (1 Cor. 11:18–19).

The second-century Christians viewed a divisive or schismatic person very dimly. But they didn't condemn someone who innocently misunderstood a passage of Scripture. Being divisive constituted heresy in the original sense of the word. Making a theological error did not. But just as the Christian theologians have changed the word "doctrine" to mean theology, they have also changed the word "heresy" to mean theological error.

The early children of the kingdom placed little emphasis on defined dogma because they well understood that the essence of Christianity was not theology—but *relationship*. It's an obedient love-faith relationship with Jesus Christ that produces genuine Christian fruit. It doesn't take much theology to enter into such a relationship with Christ. And Christ, like His Father, is a gentle teacher, who "is ready to make the most of what we say correctly" and to overlook the things we understand only dimly. The two great commandments on which the Law and the Prophets hung were not theology and religiosity but loving God with our whole heart, soul, and mind and loving our neighbor as ourselves. The kingdom of God hangs on the same two commandments.

The second-century church was by no means perfect, and neither was the first-century church. But the second-century church was still a church populated primarily by children of the kingdom. Things began changing in the third century, yet it was still a decidedly kingdom-oriented church, a church that focused on fruit. Nevertheless, the third century did give birth to the first Christian who can truly be called a theologian.

8

The Rise of Theologians

The people who have done the most harm to Christianity have invariably been people who were actually trying to help the cause of Christ. From what I've observed, few people have purposely tried to corrupt Christianity. The people who have introduced innovations have almost always thought that they were doing the work of God. So it should come as no surprise that the first Christian theologian was a godly man who devoted his entire life to Jesus Christ and His kingdom. His name was Origen. In fact, Origen had no further aim in life than to serve Christ and be a fellow worker in the kingdom.

Origen nearly lost his life in persecution when he was only seventeen, and as an older man, he faithfully endured torture for the name of Christ. In fact, he died as a result of his imprisonment and torture. Actually, in most ways, Origen personified the kingdom life taught by Jesus on the Sermon on the Mount. He witnessed about Christ to whomever he could. He passed up wealth to live in poverty for the King. And he always treated both friend and foe alike with gentleness and love.

Now I realize that my description may portray a different Origen than you've heard about in books and pamphlets. Today, Origen is blamed for just about every heresy imaginable. He's even erroneously blamed for the Alexandrine text used in modern Bible translations. However, what I usually find is that the people who criticize or condemn Origen have never read one word of his writings. They know nothing about his godly lifestyle and the close walk he had with Christ. All they know about him are things they've read in pamphlets and books about him.

Although Origen was a man of God, he had one major attribute that proved to be as much of a curse to him as it was a blessing. That attribute was that he was a genius. And it proved to be his undoing. One might say that Origen was the Leonardo da Vinci or Isaac Newton of his day. If he had devoted his life to science, who knows what discoveries he might have made. Like most geniuses, he had unlimited curiosity and boundless energy.

Origen took on Christianity's toughest critics and silenced them with his answers. He even carried on correspondence with the wife of one of the Roman emperors. Although he was from Alexandria, Egypt, he traveled throughout Palestine to learn as much about the geography of the area as he could. He became the first Biblical geographer. He dialogued with prominent Jewish theologians of his day. In fact, he was the first Gentile Christian to actually learn Hebrew. He did this so he could better defend the faith against the ridicule the Jews were heaping on it.

Most of the pamphlets and books written today in support of the King James Version attack Origen and accuse him of tampering with the Scriptures and creating the Alexandrine text. However, it is not the Alexandrine text that follows Origen's recommended readings. Rather, it is the Majority Text and the Textus Receptus, from which the King James Version was translated.*

The First Doctrinal Textbook

It's too bad that Origen didn't limit his intellectual gifts to textual criticism, Biblical geography, and defending Christianity against the attacks made by the Romans and Jews. If he had so limited himself, his spiritual legacy would have remained untarnished. However, Origen's unbridled intellectual curiosity sent him down paths he should never have entered.

One of the great mistakes Origen made was to write Christianity's first theological work. It was a book entitled *On First Principles.* Since Origen's day, so many theological books have been written on the "basic doctrines of Christianity," that we now take such doctrinal books for granted. But that's because of the precedent Origen set. In his day, it was a novel idea.

The New Testament had always been the book that contained the fundamentals of the faith. There was no need for any human work in addition to it. Christianity had prospered for nearly 200 years without a doctrinal textbook, so why start some-

---

* The reliance of the Textus Receptus on Origen's textual recommendations is detailed in my audio CD, "The Early Christian Writings and the Textus Receptus," available from Scroll Publishing Co.

thing new? By writing a doctrinal textbook, Origen was implying that the New Testament is insufficient.

Now, if Origen had limited his work to merely summarizing the body of beliefs handed down to Christians of his day, it might not have been a particularly bad idea. However, the purpose of his book was not to reiterate what the church already taught. No, the purpose of *On First Principles* was to speculate on theological areas for which the church had no set teachings and where the Bible sheds little light. In other words, it was largely a work of personal theological speculation.

For example, in his book Origen discussed the question of where we get our souls. Do they exist before they are given to our bodies? Or are they created anew at the moment of conception? Do our parents create our soul in conception? Or does God make a special creation every time a human is conceived? The church had no teaching on the subject because the Bible has no teaching on it. There are many areas about life and eternity that the Bible simply doesn't tell us much about. The wise thing is to leave those things alone and not delve into mysteries that God hasn't chosen to reveal to us.

Unlike the doctrinal books written after his day, Origen wasn't trying to tell other Christians what *they* should believe. He made it clear that what he wrote were simply his personal speculations. He always set forth what the church said on each subject, and he was careful not to contradict what the church taught. His inquiries were limited to areas in which the church had no teaching. Origen was only in his twenties when he wrote *On First Principles*. He was a young man who held no position of authority in the church, and the furthest thing from his mind was to make dogmatic assertions about what others must believe. Nevertheless, *On First Principles* is the work that launched the new class of Christian theologians.

Instead of simply sticking to the language of Scripture—and leaving things alone that are not revealed—Origen set the precedent of going beyond Scripture. He made it acceptable to speculate about things for which we have been given no clear revelation. He also helped to create a rift between the "wise and educated" and the ordinary Christian. The learned could understand and dialogue about Origen's theological speculations. The ordinary Christians couldn't. It was like the Jewish theologians versus the ordinary, uneducated Jews.

Once Origen opened the door, a wave of theological speculation followed. And before the third century was over, Christians everywhere were entangled in theological speculations and disputes. Whereas Origen had a kind, undogmatic spirit, the theologians who followed him were often dogmatic and judgmental.

The First Commentaries

Origen has the distinction of writing not only the first theological treatise but also the first set of commentaries. But his commentaries further amplified the notion that the "ordinary and uneducated" were merely skimming the surface of the Scriptures. His commentaries promoted the idea that there was a lot of spiritual meat average Christians were missing and that only the "wise and prudent" could grasp. And that notion has continued to this very day. Nowadays the typical Christian who is asked to teach Sunday School or preach a message thinks he has to turn to a commentary to be able to understand what the Scriptures are "really" saying.

After Origen's death, the balance of power in the church shifted away from the ordinary and uneducated to the "wise and prudent." A new class of theologians had formed. Although Origen unwittingly launched the Christian theological movement, he himself remained a kingdom Christian his entire life. He never lost sight of the kingdom. Sadly, the same cannot be said about those who followed him.

9

The First Theological Brawl

It's important to understand that the theologians attained their ascendancy over the church in stages. It didn't happen all at once. Rather, it took about 150 years after the death of Origen before the church regressed to essentially the same situation the Jews were in at the time of Christ. None of the key figures involved in establishing the new class of theologians were purposely trying to harm the church. Most of them were trying to "save the church" from heretics. Nevertheless, these well-intentioned men created something that was in direct opposition to what Jesus had established for His kingdom.

By the beginning of the fourth century, the church was embroiled in theological wars. These wars were engendered by two things: (1) Christians were speculating on things they should have left alone and (2) they had lost their focus on Christ the King and His kingdom. They were placing theological dogma above kingdom fruit.

One theological battle in particular came to the center stage. It's generally known today as the Arian controversy. It concerned the begetting of the Son. The Scriptures merely tell us that Jesus is the "only begotten of the Father" and that He existed as the Word "in the beginning" (Jn. 1:1,14).

Nevertheless, the church did have a uniform teaching about the Son and His eternal generation from the Father. They likened the Father, Son, and Holy Spirit to our sun. The Father is like the sun itself. The Son is like the beams of light begotten by the sun.* The Holy Spirit is like the heat that proceeds from the sun.

If our sun were eternal, then so would be the light and heat that come from it. Similarly, since the Father is eternal, so are the Son and Holy Spirit. The Scriptures tell us that all of the fullness of Godhood or the Divine nature dwell in Jesus. So He has the same nature as the Father. At the same time, the Scriptures clearly state that the Father is the head of Christ. The Father and Son are equal in nature; yet, there is a hierarchy of headship or order within the Trinity.†

Now, the second-century Christians never felt that having a complete understanding of the Trinity was one of the essentials of the faith. That's why their

---

* Heb. 1:3 calls the Son the "brightness" or radiance of the Father's glory.

† "I want you to know that the head of every man is Christ, the head of woman is man, and the head of Christ is God" (1 Cor. 11:3). "I have not spoken on My own authority; but the Father who sent Me gave Me a command, what I should say and what I should speak" (Jn. 12:49,50). "When all things are made subject to Him, then the Son Himself will also be subject to Him who put all things under Him, that God may be all in all" (1 Cor. 15:25–28).

statement of belief simply stated: "I believe in only one God Almighty, the Creator of the universe, and His Son Jesus Christ."

How the Brawl Started

But the fourth century church was considerably different from the second-century church. By the fourth century, the church was filled with amateur theologians who thought they needed to nail down matters that are not explicit in Scripture. To this end, Alexander, the bishop of Alexandria, had called together all the elders in the city and put forward to them questions about the begetting of the Son and His relationship to the Father.

From the views Alexander expressed during his questioning, one of the elders named Arius became convinced that Alexander held to an unorthodox view of the Father and the Son. It seemed to Arius that Alexander held to a position that is often called Sabellianism or Modalism. Today, it's better commonly known as Oneness theology. It's the view that the Father and Son are merely different modes of the same person. So Arius quickly contradicted what Alexander was teaching on the subject, and the two men got into a heated argument. The other elders joined one side or the other, and soon what had begun as a personal controversy engulfed the entire Christian population of Alexandria. From there, it spilled over to other churches.

Arius committed the classic theological mistake that I refer to as Newton's law of theology. Newton's third law of motion states that for every action there is an equal and opposite reaction. In theology, whenever someone promotes a theological error, someone else usually reacts by going to the opposite extreme—creating a new theological error in response.

Arius was so determined to counteract the Oneness error that he swung way too far in the other direction. He ignored what the church had always taught about the Father and the Son and claimed that because the Son is begotten, it must mean that He came into existence at some point. He also said that the Son was created out of nothing— disregarding the church's teaching that the Son is eternally begotten from the Father, as light is begotten from the sun. Caught up in his own sense of self-importance, Arius didn't care if he tore the church apart in his attempt to rescue it from the Oneness error.

Just Drop It!

Constantine was convinced that Christianity was the one true religion, and he wanted to advance its cause. However, he was chagrined when he learned that as a result of his granting Christians religious freedom, they were now fighting among themselves. So he conferred with one of the most respected bishops in the church, Hosius of Spain. Hosius explained to Constantine the nature of the controversy, and the solution he recommended was straightforward: Tell both sides simply to drop the matter.

So Constantine wrote a letter addressed to Alexander and Arius, and Hosius traveled to Egypt to personally deliver the letter and to encourage the two men to follow the advice in it. The letter said in part:

> What then is our advice? It is this: That it was wrong in the first instance to propose such questions as these. Or to reply to them when propounded. For those points of discussion are not required by the authority of any law. Rather, they are suggested by the contentious spirit that is fostered by misused free time.
>
> Even though they may be intended merely as an intellectual exercise, they certainly should be confined to the region of our own thoughts, and not hastily produced in the popular assemblies, nor unadvisedly entrusted to the general ear. For how very few are there who are able either to accurately comprehend or to adequately explain subjects so sublime and obscure in their nature.[1]

That was the voice of wisdom speaking: Just drop it and focus on following Christ! Don't speculate on matters that aren't specifically defined in Scripture. It was the voice of plain, primitive, fruit-oriented Christianity. But it was one of the last times that voice would be heard.

Drop It?

"Drop it? But that would've caused all sorts of horrible things to come into the church!" I hear people say today. "Didn't Hosius see what that does to the nature of the Son?"

Yes, Hosius understood perfectly well what it does to the nature of the Son: It does nothing. Whether or not the matter had been dropped, the nature of the Son remains the same. Or are we so foolish as to imagine that our conceptions about the nature of the

Son's begetting and His relationship to the Father have any bearing on the reality of those things? The divinity of the Father and the Son and their true nature and relationship remain the same regardless of what we ignorant humans may think.

The average, unlearned Christian of the second century probably couldn't have given a completely correct explanation of the begetting of the Son or of the relationship of the Father and Son. Some Christians erroneously held to the Oneness error, thinking that the Father was the Son. But no councils were convened and no one was excommunicated over this error. The second-century church simply left the matter alone. What were the results? Did there cease to be a Father and a Son because some Christians misunderstood Jesus' words? Of course not.

But, as I said, the fourth-century church was different. So nobody heeded Hosius' advice to drop the whole matter. Although we can't say for certain what would have happened if everyone had agreed to drop the issue, we do know for certain what happened because they refused to drop it. And the damage to the kingdom was catastrophic.

10

The Major Turning Point in Christian History

When the parties involved refused to drop the issue, Constantine came up with the idea of convening a council of as many bishops as possible at his summer capital of Nicaea. He hoped such a worldwide council would be able to settle the issue.

Outside of the events covered in the New Testament, the Council of Nicaea was without a doubt the major turning point in all of Christian history. It was a much more momentous turning point than even the Reformation. That's because it opened a Pandora's box that has never been closed.

The Adequacy of Scripture

The reason Constantine convened the council was to bring Christians together, not to further divide them. So when the delegates arrived, Constantine urged them to try to find common ground they could agree on. Accordingly, different men proposed that the delegates come up with a formula of belief that everyone present could accept. Several proposals were made, using only the language of Scripture.

The supporters of Arius were agreeable to these formulas.

But now events took a new turn. Even though the proposed formulas were completely orthodox and followed the language of Scripture, the party of Alexander rejected them. Why? Because they knew that in the recesses of their minds, the Arians meant something different than the party of Alexander when they recited these formulas. The point of the council had now changed. Its purpose was no longer to recover an erring brother or to create a Scriptural formula that would end the fighting. No, the objective now was to drive a wedge between the Arian party and the Alexandrine party by coming up with a formula that the Arians couldn't accept.

At the same time, the party of Alexander realized that they had reached the limits of Scripture. Instead of accepting this limitation, they made a momentous decision. They decided that the Scriptures were simply inadequate. The council must go *beyond* Scripture if it was going to force the Arians out of the church.

Constantine saw that the majority of the delegates were now supporting Alexander, so in exasperation he himself gave up on the goal of achieving unity among all the delegates. He himself now proposed a statement of belief that would force the Arians out of the church and end the matter. But to do this, he had to insert language in the creed that is not found in Scripture. Constantine's proposal won the day, and it was accepted by nearly everyone at the council—except Arius and a few of his staunchest supporters. This creed is known today as the Nicene Creed, and it reads:

> We believe in one God, the Father Almighty, Maker of all things visible and invisible; and in one Lord Jesus Christ, the Son of God, the only-begotten of His Father, of the substance of the Father, God of God, Light of Light, true God of true God, begotten, not made, being of the same substance with the Father; by whom all things were made, both that are in heaven and in earth; who for us men and for our salvation came down from heaven, was incarnate and was made man. He suffered and the third day he rose again, and ascended into heaven. And he shall come again to judge both the living and the dead. And we believe in the Holy Spirit.[1]

Homoousian

Now the Nicene Creed is completely orthodox in its meaning. This is obvious from the writings of the various delegates who were at the council. These men were simply affirming that the Son is eternal and that He is of the same nature as His Father. This summarizes the historic faith, and for that reason I subscribe to the Nicene Creed. Nevertheless, I decry the spirit of Nicaea and the fruit that it produced. The council could have simply removed Arius from office and excommunicated him from the Church for being a divisive man and for teaching contrary to the faith once handed down. They didn't have to create a new creed to do this.

I also fault the Nicene Creed for introducing a new theological term, *homoousian,* in the phrase, "being of the same substance with the Father." This new term combines two Greek words, *homo*, meaning "same," and *ousia*, meaning "substance." In fact, after Nicaea the term *homoousian* became the primary touchstone of orthodoxy.

But there is a serious problem with this word: It nowhere appears in Scripture. So the council was now saying that to be a Christian you now *had* to subscribe to a theological term that nowhere appears in the Bible. Actually even the word *ousia*, which does appear in Scripture, is never used in the Bible with reference to God.[2]

So the winners at Nicaea were saying that Scripture alone is not adequate to settle disputes. They were also saying that the Bible doesn't fully explain or define certain matters that we *need* to know.

Christianity Becomes Doctrianity

The strong message that came from the Council of Nicaea is that God's grace will cover all manner of wicked living, but it will not cover theological errors. God suddenly became someone who is more concerned about our theology than our fruit. And this was despite the fact that Jesus told us, "Every sin and blasphemy will be forgiven men, but the blasphemy against the Spirit will not be forgiven men. Anyone who speaks a word against the Son of Man, it will be forgiven him" (Mt. 12:31, 32).

The reality that a person bore the fruits from an obedient love-faith relationship with Christ no longer carried any weight. On the other hand, even though someone bore none of the fruit that comes from a real relationship with Christ, he was still accepted as a Christian and was quite welcome in the church—so long as he held to the Nicene Creed.

The word heretic—which originally meant a schismatic person—now came to mean a person who held to a defined theological error. And heretics were painted as the embodiment of evil. In short, Christianity had become Doctrianity.

11

When Theologians Rule

Interestingly, the new class of Christian theologians used the same two methods perfected by the Jewish theologians to maintain their power: (1) language bullying and (2) a claim to a special status as the official interpreters of Scripture.

The writings of the second-century Christians contain virtually no discussions or wrangling over the meaning of particular Greek words used in the Scriptures. However, in the fourth century, much of the theological fighting was over the meaning of the Greek used by the New Testament writers. It never occurred to any of the parties that perhaps some Greek words had changed their meaning in the centuries that had passed since the age of the apostles.

As I've mentioned, the Nicene creed centered on a special theological term not even found in Scripture: *homoousian.* Furthermore, the fourth-century theologians began creating new specialized definitions of Greek words used in Scripture. But what did this do to the ordinary, uneducated Greek-speaking Christians? It marginalized them. They basically had to shut up and listen to the new theologians because they were in no position to try to argue linguistics against the elite.

If the theologians marginalized and bullied ordinary Greek-speaking Christians, imagine what they did to the average Latin-speaking and Aramaic-speaking Christians. Because most of the theological battles of the fourth and fifth centuries were fought with newly formed theological Greek terms, the many Christians who couldn't speak Greek were easily cowed into submission.

Missing the Big Picture

As it turned out, the theological battles started by Alexander and Arius were not settled by the Nicene council. The two sides waged war (both literally and figuratively) for more than a century after Nicaea. Eventually the Nicene party won the battle. But they lost the war for the kingdom. By the time the Arian controversy was entirely over, Christianity bore little resemblance to the Christianity that had flourished before the controversy began. The theologians proved themselves to be blind guides, straining at a gnat and swallowing a camel.

Like the Jewish theologians before them, the new class of Christian theologians never understood that the way we most effectively honor God is through an obedient love-faith relationship with Him. Instead, they vainly imagined that we honor God primarily through our theological views, not the fruit evident in our lives.

It's interesting to note that in the centuries after Nicaea, no one was ever burned at the stake or dragged before the Inquisition because he wasn't producing kingdom fruit. Rather, people were tortured, imprisoned, and burned at the stake for holding to heretical beliefs (real or imagined), possessing copies of Scripture, holding unauthorized Christian meetings, or preaching without a license. If a person can't see how totally despicable it is in the eyes of Christ to torture others, burn them alive, or kill them in some other way—that person is truly blind.

Adding Human Teaching to God's Word

When the Christian theologians came into power, they quickly started adding human teaching to God's Word—as had the scribes and Pharisees. We've discussed how the bishops at the Council of Nicaea made "orthodox" Christianity turn on a word not even found in Scripture. But that was only the beginning. They soon began claiming that the decision of the Nicene council was inspired by God and stood on the same level as Scripture. Even worse, they began undermining the very teachings of Jesus Himself.

12

What Happened While the Theologians Wrangled

As I mentioned earlier, the last voice of the early Christians was the admonition from bishop Hosius to drop the whole matter. Christians today have a hard time understanding that advice. Yet the wisdom of that advice becomes clear when we look at what happened because everyone decided to continue the dispute.

I've stated that the council of Nicaea ended up being *the* great turning point in Christian history. And it was a turning point for evil, not for good. Ironically, the Nicene council didn't even accomplish what it was convened to do. That is, it didn't end the Arian controversy. Rather, it widened it. The conflict raged on for over a century more. While the church leaders were so absorbed with the Arian issue, they allowed all sorts of serious corruptions to enter the church. Here are just a few of them.

Union of Church and State

The delegates to the Nicene council were so wrapped up in the theological issues before them that not one of them questioned the propriety of an unbaptized Roman emperor convening a council of Christian bishops. Nor did they question this secular ruler's *presiding* at the council. They even accepted the creed he proposed, although it went beyond Scripture.

Although Constantine had involved himself in church affairs before Nicaea, it was the Nicene Council that effectively united church and state. Yet, the church leaders were so caught up in the Arian dispute that none of them took any notice of this momentous change. They imagined they had the insight to solve *divine* questions, yet they couldn't even manage earthly ones. And none of them saw the impossibility of uniting the kingdom of God with the kingdoms of this world. They thought they could turn the Roman empire into the kingdom of God. They somehow couldn't grasp one of the rudimentary facts about the kingdom: that it is "not of this world" (Jn. 18:36).

Persecution

Hand in hand with church and state union came persecution of those whom the church opposed. Somehow the victorious bishops at Nicaea took no note that the punishment meted out to Arius was not censure or excommunication—it was exile to the remote regions of the Roman empire. Actually, the bishops accepted this state-enforced punishment with glee. In persecuting someone who held to theological errors, their actions did more to dishonor Christ than did the theological errors of Arius. But somehow this never occurred to them.

However, exile was only the beginning. Immediately after Nicaea, Constantine issued an edict ordering all copies of Arius' writings to be burned, and he pronounced the *death penalty* for anyone caught harboring Arius' writings thereafter. Yet, there was not so much as one whimper of protest from the leaders of the church. Before the fourth century was over, the Spanish Christian, Priscillian, and six of his followers were put to death for promoting ascetic disciplines. Persecution of the Priscillianists was soon followed by persecution of the Donatists.

Interestingly, blasphemy became one of the favorite words of the new theologians, just as it had been a pet word of the Jewish theologians of old. (Mt. 26:65, Mk. 14:64, Jn. 10:33). However, in their blindness, the theologians didn't see that their murdering others in the name of God was far more blasphemous than the errors of the various heretics (real or imagined) they persecuted.

Us and Them

Please note that Jesus didn't tell His disciples that some of *you* will put your fellow Christians to death, thinking you're doing God an act of service. Rather, He said, "The time is coming that whoever *kills you* will think that he offers God service" (Jn. 16:2). So it is never the disciples of Christ who do the killing. They are the ones *being killed.* The ones doing the killing are always a third party—someone outside the kingdom. On the same note, Jesus said, "When *they* persecute you in this city, flee to another" (Mt. 10:23). Real Christians are the ones who are persecuted. They're never the ones who do the persecuting (Phil. 1:29).

Accordingly, when professing Christians kill and persecute others, they've taken themselves out of

God's kingdom (if they were ever there to start with) and have included themselves among "them." They have become outsiders—people who no longer belong to Christ. And that is precisely what the Christian theologians did from the fourth century on. Just like the Jewish theologians, the Christian theologians murdered—not only genuine heretics—but also some true children of the kingdom. And they imagined they had done an act of service in the process. They dreamed they were honoring God.

To persecute and murder fellow Christians because of their beliefs was an utter denial of Christ and everything His kingdom stands for. In the parable of the faithful and evil servant, Jesus stated quite emphatically how He felt about Christians persecuting their brethren:

> If that evil servant says in his heart, 'My master is delaying his coming,' and begins to beat his fellow servants, and to eat and drink with the drunkards, the master of that servant will come on a day when he is not looking for him and at an hour that he is not aware of, and will cut him in two and appoint him his portion with the hypocrites. There shall be weeping and gnashing of teeth (Mt. 24:48–51).

In short, Jesus is not going to put up with professing Christians who beat (let alone kill) their fellow Christians. Yet, despite the introduction of this ghastly practice under their watch, the theologians of the fourth century turned a blind eye to it. They were much too busy sniffing out any vestiges of Arianism.

War and Violence

From the very beginning, Christians had always renounced war, violence, and killing of every sort. The writings of the early Christians make this clear.[*] Even the Council of Nicaea ruled that ex-soldiers who went back into the military were to be excommunicated.[1]

However, within a few years after Nicaea, Christians began joining the army. At first, "Christians" only warred against pagans, but before the century was over, "Christians" were slaughtering fellow "Christians." It wasn't just Catholics against Arians, but also Catholics against Catholics and Arians against Arians.

---

[*] "We who formerly murdered one another now refrain from making war even upon our enemies" (Justin Martyr, 1.176). "We have learned not to return blow for blow, nor to go to law with those who plunder and rob us. Instead, even to those who strike us on one side of the face, we offer the other side also" (Athenagoras, 2.129). "The Christian does no harm even to his enemy (Tertullian, 3.51). "God puts His prohibition on every sort of man-killing by that one inclusive commandment: 'You shall not kill'" (Tertullian, 3.80).

"To those who inquire of us from where we come, or who is our founder, we reply that we have come agreeably to the counsels of Jesus. We have cut down our hostile, insolent, and wearisome swords into plowshares. We have converted into pruning hooks the spears that were formerly used in war. For we no longer take up 'sword against nation,' nor do we 'learn war anymore.' That is because we have become children of peace for the sake of Jesus, who is our Leader" (Origen, 4.558). "Christians do not attack their assailants in return, for it is not lawful for the innocent to kill even the guilty" (Cyprian, 5.351). (All references are to the volumes and pages of the *Ante-Nicene Fathers*.)

Once professing Christians decided that violence was a justifiable means to settle issues, they didn't limit it to war. Mobs of Christians fought and killed each other over the election of bishops and other issues. They murdered a pagan philosopher in Alexandria, and they burned down a Jewish synagogue in the remote eastern Roman city of Callinicum.

Yet, once again, the theologians were too busy worrying about the Arians to take any notice of this. When they did finally take notice, theologians such as Augustine tried to argue that war is compatible with Christ's teachings. For example, Augustine wrote:

> It may be supposed that God could not authorize warfare, because in later times it was said by the Lord Jesus Christ, "I say unto you that you resist not evil. But if anyone strikes you on the right cheek, turn to him the left also." However, the answer is that what is required here is not a *bodily* action, but an *inward* disposition.[2]

So according to Augustine, so long as you "love" the people you are killing, there is no objection to killing others in war. He continues:

> What is the evil in war? Is it the death of some who will soon die in any case, that others may live in peaceful subjection? This is mere cowardly dislike, not any religious feeling. The real evils in war are love of violence, revengeful cruelty, fierce and implacable enmity, wild resistance, the lust of power, and such things. And in obedience to God or some lawful authority, good men generally undertake wars to punish these things. That is, when force is required to inflict the punishment.[3]

The early church had completely forbidden Christians to go to war, but according to Augustine it is really an act of obedience to God to go to war. But what if a Christian serves under a wicked ruler who is in the wrong? Augustine even had an answer for that:

> There is no power but of God, who either orders or permits. Therefore, a righteous man may be serving under an ungodly king. Yet, he may perform the duty belonging to his position in the state by fighting under the order of his ruler. For in some cases it is plainly the will of God that he should fight. But, in others, this may not be so plain, for it may be an unrighteous command on the part of the king. Nevertheless, the soldier is innocent, because his position makes obedience a duty.[4]

In other words, it's not only right for Christians to war, but it's even right to war on behalf of evil rulers for a wicked cause. The sum total of Augustine's teaching and the theologians who followed after him is that there really is no kingdom of God—at least, not in this life.

The end result of such teaching is that Christians are to behave no differently than the pagan Romans. They will war against and kill one another just as the pagans had. They will persecute those they believe to be teaching error, just as the Romans had. And like the pagans, they will return evil for evil. The only difference is that instead of imagining that they are doing these things in honor of the Roman gods, they imagine that they're doing them in "love" out of honor for the real God.

13

What Else Happened Because of Nicaea

Hopefully the wisdom of Hosius' advice is now clear to you. The theologians who were trying to save the church ended up destroying it instead. But there's even more to the story.

Adulation of Mary

In his eagerness to magnify the deity of Christ, Athanasius, the most vocal defender of the Nicene Creed, gave Christ's mother Mary the title "Mother of God." After this, the fourth century witnessed an explosion in veneration of Mary, and it was the Nicene theologians—not the Arians—who took the lead in this. Augustine, the foremost defender of Nicaea in the West, gave his support to the false teachings that Mary was perpetually a virgin and that she lived a sinless life.

In fact, Augustine labeled the Christians who denied the perpetual virginity of Mary as heretics: "Heretics called anti-diacoMarianites are those who contradict the perpetual virginity of Mary and declare that after Christ was born she was joined as one with her husband."[1] In one of his sermons on the significance of Sunday, Augustine said: "It was not the visible sun, but its invisible Creator who consecrated this day for us, when the Virgin Mother, fertile of womb and integral in her virginity, brought him forth, made visible for us, by whom, when he was invisible, she too was created. A Virgin conceiving, a Virgin bearing, a Virgin pregnant, a Virgin bringing forth, a Virgin perpetual. Why do you wonder at this, O man?"[2]

When Augustine wrote that all humans sin, he excepted Mary, saying: "We must except the holy Virgin Mary, concerning whom I wish to raise no question when it touches the subject of sins, out of honor to the Lord. For from Him we know what abundance of grace for overcoming sin in every particular was conferred upon her who had the merit to conceive and bear Him who undoubtedly had no sin."[3]

Before long, the church was teaching that Mary had been bodily assumed to heaven and that she ruled as Queen of Heaven. And once again, not one whit of protest came from the lips of the Nicene theologians.

Gutting the Sermon on the Mount

While all of this was going on, prominent Nicene supporters like Augustine began explaining away Jesus' teachings in the Sermon on the Mount, as we've already seen. By the time these theologians got through with the Sermon on the Mount, the radical teachings in it had become meaningless.

For example, Jesus taught: "You have heard that it was said to those of old, 'You shall not swear falsely, but shall perform your oaths to the Lord.' But I say to you, do not swear at all" (Mt. 5:33,34). That's a straightforward commandment, and the early Christians took it literally. But Augustine had no inhibitions about contradicting his Lord:

> Let a person understand that swearing is to be reckoned not among things that are good, but among things that are necessary. Therefore, he should refrain as far as he can from indulging in it—unless by necessity. That is, when he sees men slow to believe what is useful for them to believe, unless they are assured by an oath. To this, accordingly, reference is made when it is said, "Let your speech be, Yea, yea; Nay, nay." This is good, and what is to be desired. "For whatsoever is more than these comes of evil." That is, if you are compelled to swear, know that it comes of a necessity arising from the infirmity of those whom you are trying to persuade of something.[4]

In other words, according to Augustine, Jesus' commandment was a mere *suggestion*. "Do not swear at all"—unless someone insists that you do.

Don't Turn the Other Cheek

Jesus taught: "You have heard that it was said, 'An eye for an eye and a tooth for a tooth.' But I tell you not to resist an evil person. But whoever slaps you on your right cheek, turn the other to him also" (Mt. 5:38,39). Again, this is a straightforward commandment. Or, at least it was until Augustine got through with it. But he deprived Jesus' teaching of any real meaning, saying:

We are not here precluded from inflicting such vengeance as serves for correction, and as compassion itself dictates. Nor does it stand in the way of that course proposed, where one is prepared to endure more from the hand of him whom he wishes to set right. But no one is suitable for inflicting this punishment except the man who, by the greatness of his love, has overcome that hatred that normally enflames those who wish to avenge themselves.

For it is not to be feared that parents would seem to hate a little son when, on committing an offence, he is beaten by them so that he may not go on offending. And certainly the perfection of love is set before us by the imitation of God the Father Himself. . . . "For whom the Lord loves He corrects. Yes, He scourges every son whom He receives." The Lord also says, "The servant who knows not his Lord's will, and does things worthy of stripes, shall be beaten with few stripes; but the servant who knows his Lord's will, and does things worthy of stripes, shall be beaten with many stripes.". . .

From this source the most suitable example is drawn, in order that it may be sufficiently clear that sin can be punished in love rather than be left unpunished. Accordingly, one may actually wish that the person on whom he inflicts punishment not to be made miserable because of the punishment. Rather, he desires him to be happy by means of the correction.[5]

So it is okay to take vengeance on an assailant, after all. Only make sure you do it out of love, in order to correct the person! With such mental gymnastics, a person can make any verse of the Bible say whatever he wants it to say.

Imagine! With their lips the Nicene theologians exalted Jesus as highly as possible. But in reality, they didn't hesitate to contradict His very words. They gutted His teachings, corrupted His kingdom, murdered others, and altered the historic faith handed down to them. But—like the Jewish theologians before them—they imagined that God was beaming down at them with eyes of delight.

Yes, the Nicene theologians ably defended the eternal begetting of the Son. It took more than a century to root Arianism (or what was called Arianism) out of the Roman people and nearly another century to root it out of the Germanic tribes. But while these theologians were devoting all of their energy to expunging Arianism from the institutional church, Christianity was so thoroughly corrupted that it bore only a faint resemblance to the Christianity of the apostolic age.

The theologians had won the battle, but lost the war. Nevertheless, as a result of the Arian controversy, the theological class became deeply entrenched in a position of power that they hold to this day.

14

The Problem with Doctrianity

In the aftermath of Nicaea, Jesus' words, "follow me" were no longer the focus of the institutional church. It was now "study me." And that is a real problem. For Doctrianity requires no real relationship with Christ and no fruit. It requires only a change in our heads, not a change in our hearts. A Pharisee can easily embrace Doctrianity. But he will never be able to embrace Christianity without a thorough change of heart.

Although the Catholics and Arians waged bitter war against each other (with both verbal and physical swords), in reality they both embraced the same religion: the religion of Doctrianity. By their actions, both sides showed themselves to be devoid of the spirit of Christ.

The eighteenth-century Christian writer, William Law, made a perceptive observation about Catholics and Protestants in his day:

> Catholics and Protestants have hated, fought, and killed one another for the sake of their different opinions, yet they have been in the highest union and communion with one another as to the lust of the

flesh, the lust of the eye, and the pride of life. This is why Christendom, full of the nicest sayings about faith, grace, works, merits, satisfactions, heresies, schisms, and so on, is also full of all the evil tendencies that prevailed in the pagan world when none of the things of God were ever thought of.[1]

William Law could have just as accurately written the same thing about the Catholics and Arians. For both sides had been converted to Doctrianity. Although they disagreed on the eternal begetting of the Son, they were in utmost agreement and communion when it came to wickedness, total ignorance about the kingdom of God, and lack of godly fruit.

Both the Catholics and Arians were in complete agreement that they knew more than the faithful Christians who had preceded them. They were of one mind that the essence of Christianity was theology, not an obedient love-faith relationship with Christ. They were in complete agreement that church and state should be unified and that it was right to persecute and murder heretics.

Dog Meat for Children

During the mid-fourth century—while the Great Theological Brawl was at its height—a man named Ulfilas brought Christianity (or rather, Doctrianity) to the pagan Goths, a Germanic tribe that lived beyond the Danube River.

History books often erroneously state that Ulfilas was an Arian. However, we have the statement of belief that he brought to the Goths, and it is certainly not Arian. The problem is that Athanasius, the great defender of Nicaea, labeled everyone who wouldn't accept the Nicene Creed as Arian, even though they had no connection with Arius. The truth is that Ulfilas and tens of thousands like him were neither Arian nor Nicene, but held to an independent understanding of Christ's nature that was biblical.

However, ultimately, it hardly matters—for the religion of nearly everyone in the fourth century who professed Christianity was actually Doctrianity. The following episode makes this clear.

In the summer and fall of A.D. 376, tens of thousands of displaced Christian Goths and other tribes arrived at the banks of the Danube River in great need. The armies of the Huns were devastating their lands and slaughtering tens of thousands of them. They asked their Christian brothers, the Romans, for permission to cross the Danube and settle within the boundaries of the Roman Empire. The Huns had no boats with which to pursue them once they crossed the river.

The Roman emperor Valens allowed them to settle within the Roman Empire if they would serve as confederates of the Romans, to which the Goths agreed. The emperor promised the Goths farming land, food, and protection. Although the Roman commanders overseeing the migration of the Goths into the Roman Empire were professing Christians, they would not let the weak, old, and sickly cross the Danube. Instead, these helpless people were left to starve or else be slaughtered by the Huns.

Contrary to their word, the Christian Romans provided the Christian Goths with neither sufficient food nor adequate land to grow their own food. Before long, the Goths were facing extreme starvation. Instead of helping them, the Romans herded the Goths into a temporary holding area surrounded by the Roman armies. Because there was only enough food to feed the Roman soldiers, the Romans heartlessly forced the Goths into a cruel alternative: either they could starve to death or they could sell their children as slaves to the Romans in exchange for dog meat.

When even more treacherous events followed, the Goths rose up in desperation against the "Christian" Romans. At the battle of Adrianople in A.D. 378, the Goths decisively defeated their Roman tormenters, slaughtering Emperor Valens along with most of his Roman army. After their victory, the Goths roamed at will throughout the Roman countryside, plundering towns, villages, and farms.

Although these Goths later entered into a temporary peace with the Romans, eventually the armies of other Christian Goths ended up sacking Rome. Yes, the so-called "barbarians" who overthrew the Roman Empire were nearly all professing Christians. At that point in time, it made little difference whether someone was Catholic, Arian, or something in between. The religion they all embraced was Doctrianity. It was a religion that placed great emphasis on head knowledge, but little emphasis on the indwelling of Christ.

Call them what you like, but please don't call them followers of Jesus. His followers don't leave the sick and elderly to die. They don't force others to sell their children in exchange for dog meat. And—although I'm very sympathetic to the Goths—I must also say that followers of Jesus don't retaliate against their oppressors by slaughtering and plundering them.

15

Luther: Theologian in Sheep's Clothing

Today many Christians mistakenly believe that the Reformation changed that whole mess. They think that the Reformation brought about a return to genuine Christianity. But in reality the Reformation merely exchanged a new form of Doctrianity in place of the old form.

Martin Luther was totally blind to the real disease infecting the church. He didn't recognize that the disease was Doctrianity. Luther thought that the problem was simply *wrong* theology. He imagined that if he substituted right theology for wrong theology, then Christianity would be back where it started. And he thought that apostolic Christianity would automatically be restored by the adoption of his new doctrines.

As a result, the Reformation was merely a battle between old theology versus new theology. Neither the Catholics nor the Reformers taught a Christianity that required fruit. They both worshiped at the altar of Doctrianity.

The English spiritual giant, William Law, described the kind of Christianity that such a focus on theology creates:

He who places any value in theological arguments or opinions that are held about the biblical doctrines of faith, justification, sanctification, election, and reprobation, depart from the true worship of the living God within him. In fact, he sets up an idol of ideas to be worshipped. . . .

I believe that every group of Christians whose religion stands upon this ground, however ardent their zeal may seem to be in such matters, will sooner or later find that their evil, ungodly nature is at the bottom of it. They will soon enough discover a selfish, earthly, overbearing pride in their own definitions and doctrines.[1]

Luther the Arrogant

William Law's prediction of what would happen to persons who put faith in theological arguments was aptly demonstrated in the life of Martin Luther. He undeniably had a "selfish, earthly, overbearing pride" in his "own definitions and doctrines." Luther haughtily belittled anybody—ancient or contemporary—who disagreed with his novel doctrine of easy believism. Not only that, but he arrogantly sneered at Scripture when it dared to contradict him! He dismissed the Epistle of James as a "gospel of straw."[2] Concerning the Epistle to the Hebrews, Luther said that the worthwhile teachings in it had "wood, straw or hay mixed in with them" and that "we cannot put it on the same level with the apostolic epistles."[3]

As most Christians know, one of Luther's primary doctrines is that we're saved by faith *alone*. Yet, the Scriptures never explicitly make that statement. So Luther arrogantly took it upon himself to insert the word "alone" into the Bible. In the Epistle to the Romans, Paul wrote: "Therefore we conclude that a man is justified by faith apart from the deeds of the law" (Rom. 3:28). Luther wasn't satisfied with that statement, so he changed it to say "a man is justified by faith *alone*, apart from the deeds of the law."

When the Catholics called his hand on this, Luther refused to admit that he had overstepped the proper boundaries. Instead, he arrogantly brushed his critics aside in a public letter:

> If your papist wishes to make a great fuss about the word "alone" (*sola*), say this to him: "Doctor Martin Luther will have it so, and he says that a papist and an ass are the same thing!" I will it. I command it. My will is reason enough! For we are not going to become students and followers of the papists. Rather we will become their judge and master. We, too, are going to be proud and brag with these blockheads. And just as St. Paul brags against his madly raving saints, I will brag over these asses of mine! They are doctors? Me too. They are scholars? I am as well. They are philosophers? And I. They are dialecticians? I am too. They are lecturers? So am I. They write books? So do I.
>
> I will go even further with my bragging: I can exegete the Psalms and the Prophets, and they cannot. I can translate, and they cannot. I can read Holy Scriptures, and they cannot. I can pray, they cannot. Coming down to their level, I can do their dialectics and philosophy better than all of them put together. Plus I know that not one of them understands Aristotle. If, in fact, any one of them can correctly understand one part or chapter of Aristotle, I will eat my hat!

No, I am not overdoing it, for I have been educated in and have practiced their discipline since my childhood. I recognize how broad and deep it is. They, likewise, know that I can do everything they can do. Yet they handle me as though I were a stranger to their studies! These incurable fellows! As if I had just arrived this morning and had never seen or heard what they know and teach. How they so brilliantly parade around with their knowledge, teaching *me* what I graduated beyond twenty years ago! To all their shouting and screaming I join the harlot in singing: "I have known for seven years that horseshoe nails are iron."

So this can be the answer to your first question. Please do not give these asses any other answer to their useless braying about that word *sola* than simply: "Luther will have it so, and he says that he is a doctor above all the papal doctors." Let it remain at that. From now on, I will hold them in contempt. In fact, I have already held them in contempt, as long as they are the kind of people that they are—asses, I should say. And there are brazen idiots among them who have never learned their own art of sophistry—like Dr. Schmidt and Snot-Nose, and others like them.[4]

Quite a humble man, wasn't he?

Murdering Christ

Luther's zeal was not a zeal for the kingdom of God. Rather, it was a zeal for doctrines—his doctrines. William Law had noted: "A zeal based solely on doctrines can only do for Christians what it did for the Jews: it will murder the person and purposes of

Christ."[5] And that's exactly what Luther's zeal did: it murdered the person of Christ.

Obviously, Luther didn't have the opportunity to murder Christ personally. But he did the next worst thing—he murdered Christ's brothers, the kingdom Christians of his day. And as Jesus said, "Inasmuch as you did it to one of the least of these My brethren, you did it to Me" (Mt. 25:40).

Within a few years of Luther's rise to power, a rapidly growing group of earnest kingdom Christians rejected Luther's gospel of easy believism. That's because they realized from the Scriptures that Christ requires an obedient love-faith relationship from His disciples. These Christians taught that true followers of Christ must be children of the kingdom, living by Jesus' teachings—not in word, but in practice. They must follow Him and produce real fruit.[6] Because they baptized those believers who joined them, Luther and others called them Anabaptists, which means rebaptizers.

The respected church historian, Roland Bainton, writes about the Anabaptists:

> They challenged the whole way of life of the community. Had they become too numerous, Protestants would have been unable to take up arms against Catholics and the Germans could not have resisted the Turks. And the Anabaptists did become numerous. They despaired of society at large, but they did not despair of winning converts to their way.[7]

The common people could see that the Scriptures didn't teach Luther's gospel of easy believism, and they flocked to the Anabaptists. If people had been free to choose, perhaps the majority would have rejected Luther's interpretation of Scripture and returned to the historic faith. That is, they would have seen the necessity of maintaining an obedient love-faith relationship with Christ.

Dr. Bainton goes on to write:

> In some of the communities of Switzerland and the Rhine valley, the Anabaptists began to outnumber Catholics and Protestants alike. Would not the growth of people with such views be even more of a menace to public security than the demolition of a city wall? In 1529 the imperial meeting at Speyer declared with the concurrence alike of Catholics and Lutherans that the death penalty should be inflicted upon the Anabaptists.
>
> Menno Simons, one of their later leaders, reported the outcome: "Some they have executed by hanging, some they have tortured with inhuman tyranny, and afterwards choked with cords at the stake. Some they roasted and burned alive. Some they have killed with the sword and given them to the fowls of the air to devour. Some they have cast to the fishes."[8]

In other words, neither Luther nor the Pope were ready for professing Christians to really start following Christ in life and to live by His teachings. They feared such genuine discipleship as much as they feared the Turks. They dreaded the children of the kingdom as much as the pagan Romans had dreaded them. Like the pagan Romans, the only response they could come up with was to murder the children of the kingdom before they got any stronger.

But it wasn't only the Anabaptists whom Luther hated. He was unwilling to allow any dissent from his teachings. Luther saw that too many people were rejecting his novel gospel and accepting the gospel of Jesus. So like the theologians before him, Luther decided to squash this dissent through the armed power of the state. After all, the Lutheran Church was now the state church throughout most of the northern German states.

Luther told the German rulers: "The fact that seditious articles of doctrine should be punished by the sword needs no further proof. For the rest, the Anabaptists hold tenets relating to infant baptism, original sin, and inspiration, which have no connection with the Word of God, and are indeed opposed to it. . . . Think what disaster would ensue if children were not baptized?"[9] Luther went on to complain:

> The Anabaptists set up a ministry and congregation of their own, which is also contrary to the command of God. From all this it becomes clear that the secular authorities are bound . . . to inflict corporal punishment on the offenders. . . . Also when it is a case of only upholding some spiritual tenet, such as infant baptism, original sin, and unnecessary separation, then . . . we conclude that . . . the stubborn sectarians must be *put to death*.[10]

Luther continued this same theme in his *Exposition on Psalm 82,* saying:

> If some were to teach doctrines contradicting an article of faith, clearly grounded in Scripture and believed throughout the world by the whole Church, such as the articles that we teach children in the Creed—as, for example, if anyone would teach that Christ is not God, but a mere man, and like other prophets, as the Turks and the Anabaptists hold—such teachers should not be tolerated,

but punished as blasphemers. For they are not mere heretics, but open blasphemers, and rulers are in duty bound to punish blasphemers. . . .

Moses, in his Law, commands that such blasphemers and indeed, all false teachers, are to be stoned. So, in this case, there ought not to be much disputing, but such open blasphemers should be condemned without a hearing and without defense.[11]

Now, it was patently false that the Anabaptists taught that Christ was mere man and not fully divine. However, under Luther's policy, they were not allowed to defend themselves or even have a hearing. The rulers were to capture them and put them to death. But it wasn't really the Anabaptists they were putting to death—it was Christ.

16

How the Theologians Entrenched Themselves

We must realize that Reformation theology didn't become the dominant theology of non-Catholics because it proved victorious in the free marketplace of ideas. No, it became dominant because it was backed by the strong arm of the state.

The theologians of the Reformation and their state churches controlled the translating and printing of the Bible and other Christian works in Protestant countries. Furthermore, in all these countries, no one was allowed to preach unless he had been licensed by the state. Those who defied the state church were banished, imprisoned, or put to death.

Eventually, in Reformation states, nearly all who taught differently than the Reformers were silenced through death, torture, or imprisonment. As Luther declared:

> What I say about public preaching [by dissenters], I say even more emphatically about private preaching and secret ceremonies. These are not to be tolerated at all. . . . On peril of body and soul, no one is to listen to such a man, but report him to his pastor or his ruler.[1]

By silencing the kingdom people, the Reformers ensured that their own interpretation of Scripture would be the one that would prevail in the non-Catholic world. They then used three methods to thoroughly entrench their views so they would dominate the non-Catholic world—not only in their day, but in all generations to follow. These three methods were (1) study Bibles, (2) doctrinal textbooks, and (3) commentaries.

Study Bibles

The Catholic theologians had hindered the way into the kingdom by keeping the Bible in Latin, a language the common people could no longer understand by the Middle Ages. Luther gave the people the Bible in their own language, but he effectively blocked the entrance into the kingdom by trying to control how the people would understand the Scriptures. It would have been bad enough if Luther's only sin had been to deliberately add a word to Scripture to make it fit his theology, as I discussed earlier. But he did far more.

Luther had the audacity to add his own human commentary directly onto the pages of God's Word. Even the Jewish theologians had never been haughty enough to do that! As I've mentioned, in these comments, Luther denigrated various books of the Bible that contradicted his new theology. He told the people in his preface to the New Testament what the "real gospel" was so as to slant their interpretation of the New Testament before they even read the first word of it. He then disparaged the books of the

Bible that revealed his theology to be obviously wrong, saying:

> From all this you can now judge all the books and decide among them which are the best. John's Gospel and St. Paul's Epistles, especially that to the Romans, and St. Peter's first Epistle are the true kernel and marrow of all the books. They ought rightly be the first books and it would be advisable for every Christian to read them first and most. . . . John's Gospel is the one, understandable, true chief Gospel, far, far to be preferred to the other three and placed high above them. So, too, the Epistles of St. Paul and St. Peter far surpass the other three Gospels—Matthew, Mark, and Luke.
>
> In a word, St. John's Gospel and his first Epistle, St. Paul's Epistles—especially Romans, Galatians, and Ephesians—and St. Peter's first Epistle are the books that show you Christ and teach you all that is necessary and good for you to know—even though you were never to see or hear any other book or doctrine. Therefore St. James' Epistle is really an epistle of straw, compared to them. For it has nothing of the nature of the Gospel about it.[2]

Here Luther surpassed in audacity every theologian who had preceded him. He said a Christian can know "all that is necessary and good" about Christ without ever reading the three Gospels of Matthew, Mark, and Luke. Really? Why, these are the very Gospels that contain the bulk of Christ's teachings. What an outrageous claim! According to Luther, if you want to learn about the gospel of Jesus, go to Paul! The second-century Christians would have been stunned to hear someone say that. Yet the incredible part of all of this is that Luther actually got away with it. If today you ask the

106 Will the Theologians Please Sit Down

typical evangelical Christian what Christianity is all about, he or she will invariably take you to Romans, not to the Sermon on the Mount.

In reality, Luther took institutional Christianity one step further from the kingdom of God than had any of the theologians who preceded him. None of them had made Paul *the* master teacher of Christianity. None of them had placed Paul above Jesus.[*]

Furthermore, it wasn't just in his preface to the New Testament that Luther tried to skew his readers' viewpoints. No, he wrote individual prefaces for each of the Bible books, telling his readers what the writer of that book was "really saying" and discrediting the Bible books that contradicted his teaching.

Through his prefaces, Luther created a new thing: the study Bible. It was a hybrid—an admixture of God's Word mingled with man's word. Regrettably, when men combine God's Word with human commentary, the human commentary normally influences people more than do the words of God.

Unfortunately, most of the Bibles that came out of the Reformation and the century that followed it were study Bibles—God's Word mixed with man's word. For instance, the Bible that came to dominate the English evangelical world (until the King James Version) was the Geneva Bible, first printed in 1560. It was published in Geneva, Switzerland, under the influence of John Calvin, by English Protestants. They had fled there to escape the persecution of Queen Mary. The Geneva Bible not only contained

---

[*] As I've mentioned, the real Paul promoted Jesus' teachings. Luther's "Paul" contradicts what Jesus taught.

prefaces to each Bible book to make sure the reader would understand the Scriptures in the "proper sense," but it also contained numerous comments in the side margins to further influence and indoctrinate the reader.

From the very beginning, study Bibles have always worked to obscure the kingdom of God and the teachings of Christ. Sometimes they're subtle, and at other times they make a bold frontal attack on the kingdom.

The Geneva Bible hid the kingdom of God by telling its readers that Jesus instituted nothing revolutionary with His teachings. According to the Geneva Bible, there is no difference between Christ's moral teachings and the Law of Moses. The Geneva Bible says that Christ's teachings merely clarify matters that the Pharisees had obscured. It also says that Christ is only making clear that obedience to the Law of Moses has to begin inside our hearts and cannot be mere external obedience. Other than that, nothing has changed except the ceremonial part of the Law.[3]

With such comments all throughout the Geneva Bible, the average person would read the New Testament and never even see the kingdom of God and the radical revolution it ignited. The Geneva Bible continued to be used by evangelicals throughout the English-speaking world until it was finally surpassed in popularity by the King James Version. However, even after the publication of the King James Version, the Geneva Bible remained the Bible of the Puritans, Pilgrims, and English Separatists until the late seventeenth century.

Once the Geneva Bible lost popularity, study Bibles fell into disuse for a time. However, they had a major rebirth in the twentieth century, and now they have come to dominate the Bible publishing world. Nowadays, we have the Scofield Study Bible, the Ryrie Study Bible, the Hebrew-Greek Key Study Bible, the Open Bible, the MacArthur Study Bible, and the Zondervan NIV Study Bible, among dozens of others. There are special study Bibles for women, for teens, for charismatics, and even for children. Today, Christians have come to accept it as a natural thing to add human commentary to the pages of God's Word.[†]

Doctrinal Textbooks

The second method used by the theologians of the Reformation to make certain that their interpretation of Scripture would dominate was to publish books of systematic theology, setting forth what they claimed were the foundational doctrines of Christianity. The most successful of these by far was John Calvin's *Institutes of the Christian Religion*. It is a masterfully written work that ties all the books of Scripture together in a seemingly logical flowing stream.

Unfortunately, most of what Calvin wrote does not constitute the historic "institutes" of Christianity—any more than did the doctrinal books of Augustine. The "institutions" in Calvin's work are simply his novel inventions. But because they are

---

[†] When I speak of study Bibles, I'm not referring to simple reference Bibles that provide cross-references and explanations of coins, terms of measurement, etc.

presented in such an understandable, coherent manner, they have had an enormous influence on the Protestant world. Through his *Institutes*, Calvin presented to the Protestant world a comprehensive theological, moral, ecclesiastical, and civic system.

Regrettably, Calvin's comprehensive system completely undermined Jesus' message of the kingdom. Under Calvin's system, Christians are not supposed to be the defenseless, gentle Christians of the first three centuries. They are not to be the meek children of the kingdom who turn the other cheek and won't even take others to court. No, Calvin taught that God was still dealing with mankind just as He had in Moses' day. However, according to Calvin, instead of God's covenant being exclusively with one nation, Israel, it now can be with every nation on earth. Every country can be a potential Israel. The sixteenth century canton of Geneva was the model for how this should work.

According to Calvin, everyone in a nation needs to be brought into the covenant with God (whether they're of the elect or not) by being baptized into the covenant as infants. Statewide infant baptism should be mandatory. Ideally, a nation should be governed by the elect, just as Israel had ideally been governed by faithful priests, prophets, judges, and kings. It's the responsibility of the government to protect the church, establish and preserve the true Christian faith (i.e., Calvin's doctrines), and regulate the lives of its citizens according to God's moral law. As I've mentioned, according to Calvin, God's moral law is still the same law as that found in the Old Testament. Even the unconverted should be forced to live by the same moral laws as do converted Christians.

Essentially then, under Calvin's system, every nation can be in the same position as ancient Israel. If a nation obeys God's law, properly worships Him, and supports the teaching of true doctrine, God will prosper that nation economically and militarily. He will protect them from famines, droughts, and epidemics. If a nation is experiencing economic decline, military defeats, pestilence, and natural disasters, it means that God has a quarrel with that nation and is punishing it.

To keep this from happening, according to Calvin, the state and church must work in close partnership. For example, the state must mandate weekly church attendance for everyone. Furthermore, the local church elders or presbyters must closely examine the lives of all who attend their church to make certain all are living closely within the bounds of God's law. Although the only discipline the *church* can administer is excommunication, God expects the *state* to punish sinners in order to keep the nation pure and thereby avoid His wrath. The system that Calvin set up was not historic Christianity. Rather, it was essentially Christo-Judaism. It still had the Mosaic Law (without the "ceremonies"), a church-state combination, and national wars.

What could be further from the kingdom of God? How could anyone read the four Gospels and so totally miss Jesus' teachings about the kingdom? We can't combine His kingdom with any earthly kingdom. As Jesus made clear, "My kingdom is not of this world. If My kingdom were of this world, My servants would fight, so that I should not be delivered to the Jews" (Jn. 18:36). The ordinary, uneducated Christians of the first two centuries clearly saw that Christ's teachings made a church-state combination impossible. They also saw that Christians couldn't possibly kill non-Christians in war—let alone kill their fellow citizens of the kingdom.

But, like the fourth-century theologians, neither Luther nor Calvin ever saw the obvious contradiction between their teachings and those of Jesus. It's just as Paul said it would be: "Where is the wise? Where is the scribe? Where is the disputer of this age? Has not God made foolish the wisdom of this world?" (1 Cor. 1:20).

The most obvious things in the Scriptures are hidden from the wise. As a result, the followers of Calvin didn't hesitate to war against the Catholics. In fact, they didn't hesitate to kill each other when the goals of their respective countries differed. English Calvinists slaughtered both Scottish Calvinists and Dutch Calvinists. Some of them even killed one another in the English Civil War. Calvin's teachings had completely hidden the kingdom of God from them.

Because of the *Institutes*, Calvin ultimately surpassed Luther as the dominant theologian of the Reformation—at least in English-speaking lands. And his influence on the evangelical world remains colossal to this day. For one thing, Calvin's *Institutes* are still in print, and they are still read by theologians.

More importantly, Calvin spawned numerous copycat works by later generations of theologians. Although no single doctrinal work has had the same impact as Calvin's *Institutes of the Christian Religion*, there have been literally thousands of doctrinal textbooks written ever since by each new generation of theologians. Yet, few—if any—of these doctrinal textbooks and works of systematic theology teach the simple gospel of the kingdom. The theologians of today still imagine that theology is the essence of Christianity rather than relationship and the fruit it produces.

17

Commentaries that Muffle God's Word

One of Calvin's greatest tools for propagating his belief system was his set of commentaries on the Bible. Luther set the precedent by writing a highly influential commentary on Galatians. However, Calvin went through virtually every book of the Bible and gave his explanation of what each passage supposedly means. Through his commentaries, he was able to shape Scripture to fit his theological system. His was the first full set of commentaries written after the invention of the printing press. As a result of the printing press, his commentaries were disseminated far and wide throughout the Protestant world at an affordable cost.

To be sure, the average Reformation Christian never read Calvin's commentaries. But most evangelical preachers of his day did. As a result, so much of what was preached in evangelical pulpits throughout the world were Calvin's thoughts, not those of Jesus. In fact, Calvin had no hesitancy to explain away Jesus' words when His words didn't fit into his Christo-Judaic system. In doing this, he often plagiarized Augustine. For example, his rationalization of taking oaths comes straight from Augustine:

> JESUS: "Again you have heard that it was said to those of old, 'You shall not swear falsely, but shall perform your oaths to the Lord.' But I say to you, do not swear at all" (Matt. 5:33,34).

> CALVIN: "Many have been led by the phrase, *not at all,* to adopt the false notion that every kind of swearing is condemned by Christ. Some good men have been driven to this extreme strictness by observing the unbridled licentiousness of swearing, which prevailed in the world. The Anabaptists, too, have blustered a great deal, on the ground, that Christ appears to give no liberty to swear on any occasion, because he commands, *Swear not at all.* . . .

> Christ teaches us, in my opinion, that it originates in the wickedness of men, that they are compelled to swear: for, if honesty prevailed among men, if they were not inconsistent and hypocritical, they would maintain the simplicity that nature dictates. And yet it does not follow that it is unlawful to swear when necessity demands it. For many things are proper in themselves, though they have had a wicked origin.[1]

That, of course, is Augustine speaking, not Jesus. What about turning the other cheek? Calvin negated this teaching of Christ as well:

> JESUS: "I tell you not to resist an evil person. But whoever slaps you on your right cheek, turn the other to him also."

> CALVIN: "Unquestionably, Christ did not intend to exhort his people to whet the malice of those whose propensity to injure others is sufficiently

strong. And if they were to turn to them the other cheek, what would it be but holding out such an encouragement? It is not the business of a good and judicious commentator to eagerly seize on syllables, but to attend to the design of the speaker. And nothing is more unbecoming the disciples of Christ, than to spend time in nitpicking about words, where it is easy to see what the Master means."[2]

I see. When we take Jesus' commandments literally, we're "eagerly seizing on syllables" and "nitpicking about words."

What about loving our enemies? Calvin skillfully wiped out this teaching of Jesus as well:

JESUS: "You have heard that it was said, 'You shall love your neighbor and hate your enemy.' But I say to you, love your enemies, bless those who curse you, do good to those who hate you, and pray for those who spitefully use you and persecute you" (Mt. 5:43,44).

CALVIN: "It is obvious, as I have already said, that Christ does not introduce new laws, but corrects the wicked commentary of the Scribes, by whom the purity of the divine law had been corrupted."[3]

So Calvin adroitly sidestepped the radical implication of what Jesus said about loving our enemies. According to Calvin, Christ wasn't introducing anything new. In other words, because war was allowable under the Law, it still is allowable to Christians.

Copycat Commentaries

Although Calvin's commentaries were extremely influential in their own right, perhaps their greatest influence has been their impact on most commentaries written after them. In fact, many of the popular commentaries from the time of Calvin to the modern day have been little more than a re-working of what Calvin said.

For example, Calvin interpreted the passage about the head covering, found in the eleventh chapter of 1 Corinthians, to be addressing *public* worship. He wrote:

> It may seem, however, to be superfluous for Paul to forbid the woman to prophesy with her head uncovered, while elsewhere he wholly prohibits women from speaking in the Church. (1 Timothy 2:12.) It would not, therefore, be allowable for them to prophesy even with a covering upon their head, and hence it follows that it is to no purpose that he argues here as to a covering. It may be replied, that the Apostle, by here condemning the one, does not commend the other. For when he reproves them for prophesying with their head uncovered, he at the same time does not give them permission to prophesy in some other way, but rather delays his condemnation of that vice to another passage, namely in 1 Corinthians 14.

Although Calvin interpreted this passage to apply to public assemblies, when we read the passage under consideration (i.e., 1 Cor. 11:1–16), it makes no mention whatsoever of public assemblies. The passage that immediately precedes it (1 Cor. 10:23–33) does not concern public assemblies at all. And, as Calvin himself points out, it would be rather absurd for Paul to tell women to cover their heads when prophesying in church. That's because just a few pages later he tells them, "Let your women keep silent in the churches, for they are not permitted to speak" (1 Cor. 14:34).

Regardless, virtually every commentator ever since has followed Calvin's error. The italics are mine in the following passages:

MATTHEW HENRY: "Something like this the women of the church of Corinth seem to have been guilty of, who were under inspiration, and prayed and prophesied even in their *assemblies*."

JOHN GILL: "In this chapter the apostle blames both men and women for their indecent appearance in *public* worship."

ADAM CLARKE: "The apostle reprehends the Corinthians for several irregularities in their manner of conducting *public* worship; the men praying or prophesying with their heads covered, and the women with their heads uncovered."

ALBERT BARNES: "In regard to the first, it seems probable that some of the women who, on pretence of being inspired, had prayed or prophesied in the Corinthian *church*, had cast off their veils after the manner of the heathen priestesses."

CHARLES HODGE: "Having corrected the more private abuses which prevailed among the Corinthians, Paul begins in this chapter to consider those which relate to the way they conducted *public* worship."

JAMIESON, FAUSSET, AND BROWN: "1 Cor. 11:1–34. Censure on Disorders in Their *Assemblies.*"

PEOPLE'S NEW TESTAMENT: "Dress and Conduct *in the Church.* Summary —Men in Church to Pray with Uncovered Heads. Women to Be Veiled."

Even though the passage says nothing whatsoever about public worship and even though it renders the passage absurd to interpret it to be speaking of public assemblies (because it contradicts 1 Cor. 14), almost every commentator unthinkingly follows Calvin's error. It is truly a case of the blind leading the blind.

What I've given you is only one example. In chapter 20, we'll be looking at some other examples of copycat commentators. In the end, dead theologians like Augustine, Calvin, and Luther still rule the church from their graves.

18

Learning to Stand Up to Theological Bullies

We all know what bullies are. They are people who intimidate or hurt others as a way to obtain power, to feel important, or to get their way. Bullying is perpetrated by persons who are more powerful—either socially or physically—than their weaker victims. One encyclopedia defines bullying behavior as follows:

- The behavior is aggressive and negative.
- The behavior is carried out repeatedly.
- The behavior occurs in a relationship in which there is an imbalance of power between the two parties.
- The behavior is purposeful.[1]

Although bullying often involves physical coercion, it also can be accomplished through non-physical techniques—such as name-calling, spreading rumors, ostracism, ridicule, and arguing the victim into submission.

One writer describes adult bullies as people who are "possessed of an exceptional verbal facility and will outmaneuver most people in verbal interaction,

especially in times of conflict. They are self-opinion-
ated and display arrogance, audacity, a superior
sense of entitlement, and a sense of invulnerability
and untouchability. A bully is a control freak and
has a compulsive need to control everyone and
everything you say, do, think and believe. For example, he will launch an immediate personal attack
attempting to restrict what you are permitted to say
if you start talking knowledgeably"[2] about a subject
on which he feels he has the exclusive say. If I didn't
know better, I would have thought this writer was
giving us a description of Martin Luther.

Theological Bullies

By nature, theologians tend to be bullies. The scribes
and Pharisees certainly were. They used all of the
classical methods of bullying:

- They denigrated and ridiculed those who didn't
  follow their opinions. For example, the religious
  leaders belittled the officers who were supposed to
  arrest Jesus but failed to do so: "Are you also de-
  ceived? Have any of the rulers or the Pharisees believed in Him? But this crowd that does not know
  the Law is accursed" (Jn. 7:47–49).
- They used social ostracism, throwing those who
  crossed them out of the synagogues.
- They even resorted to physical violence, imprison-
  ing the apostles and other Christians, and murdering Jesus and faithful followers such as
  Stephen.

Unfortunately, Christian theologians have an
even worse track record than the scribes and Pharisees. They have been much more inclined to murder

and torture than even their Jewish predecessors. The famous defender of the Nicene council, Athanasius, set the pattern for all who followed him. He painted his religious foes—most of whom were not actually Arians—as the most wicked and despicable persons imaginable. He readily pronounced eternal damnation upon them. He heartily approved of their judicial exiles, and he never objected to the death penalty for those who harbored Arius' writings.

After Athanasius, the bullying got much worse. The Catholic and Orthodox churches regularly persecuted anybody who challenged the church's teaching. During the Middle Ages, genuine children of the kingdom were often imprisoned, tortured, and murdered—merely for wanting to totally follow Jesus in their lives.

The Reformers quickly demonstrated that they could be just as big bullies as the Catholics. Both Luther and Calvin were control freaks and bullies. They joined hands with the Catholics in besmirching kingdom Christians such as the Anabaptists and doing what they could to annihilate them.

Kingdom Victims

Many of the kingdom Christians who stood up to the Reformers were murdered or imprisoned in dungeons. Those who survived were forced into submission. They were driven to remote mountainous regions or distant corners of Europe. Kingdom Christians were allowed to live in a given region only on the condition that they remain quiet and not share their faith with anyone else. Consequently, they eventually became the "quiet in the land."

The centuries passed, and the children of the kingdom eventually obtained freedom of religion. But the effects and traumas through centuries of vicious bullying from the Catholics and Reformers continue to this day.

In the end, the theological bullies have largely had their way. From what I've observed, we kingdom Christians often are weak when it comes to evangelism. That's because "keeping quiet" has been deeply etched into our collective psyche. We've thrown out the bulk of our forefathers' teachings and replaced them with the doctrines of those who have bullied us. When a person reads the typical doctrinal textbooks of today's Anabaptists, Moravians, Brethren, and other kingdom Christians, he or she finds that they basically teach the doctrines of Athanasius, Augustine, Luther, and Calvin—with the mere addition of nonresistance, free will, and the head covering.

When kingdom Christians today prepare sermons and Bible lessons, they typically go to the works of the theologians—commentaries, doctrinal textbooks, and popular writings—for their insights. But why do we imagine that those who understand so little about Christ's kingdom have some inside track on understanding Scripture? On the one hand, we properly eschew seminaries and higher theological learning. But on the other hand, we go to the men of advanced learning for most of our doctrine. We continue to let the bullies dominate us.

The situation makes me think of the Israelites during the days of Samuel. The bullies at the time were the Philistines. To keep the Israelites in subjection, the Philistines outlawed all blacksmiths in Israel (1 Sam. 13:19). This kept the Israelites from making swords and spears that would enable them to stand up to the bullies. So the Israelites had to go crawling hat in hand to the Philistines to acquire any kind of needed metal instrument. Just like those ancient Israelites, we kingdom Christians today go crawling to the theologians for their doctrines and commentary on Scripture. We're afraid to stand up to the bullies.

On Commentaries and Quantum Optics

A Christian friend once told me, "The problem, David, is that when I read the New Testament I have trouble understanding what it's saying. On the other hand, when I read a commentary, then the New Testament becomes clear." Well, on the surface that seems to make sense.

If someone were to hand you a doctoral thesis on quantum optics, my guess is that you would have a hard time understanding it—unless you have an advanced degree in physics. However, I could write a line-by-line commentary on that doctoral thesis that would make it understandable to you, even if you have no background in physics. Sounds great, doesn't it?

There's only one problem: I don't know any more about quantum optics than you do. I can't even define the term! However, my ignorance of the subject wouldn't prevent me from writing a commentary on the subject that would be understandable to nonscientists. It just means that my commentary would be worthless. It would be "understandable," but it wouldn't help anyone to have any better grasp of quantum optics than he has now.

It's no different with Bible commentaries.

In theory, there's nothing wrong with the concept of a Bible commentary. The New Testament was addressed to Greek-speaking Christians living in the Mediterranean world between the years A.D. 35 to A.D. 100. I'm an English-speaking Christian living in the United States in the twenty-first century. It would be ideal to have a Bible commentary that could put me in the same position as a Greek-speaking Christian who lived in the Mediterranean world in the year A.D. 100 (when the New Testament was complete). Unfortunately, there's no commentary that does that—or that even makes a serious attempt to do it.

Standing up to Bullies

When I was in my early twenties, I had a part-time job delivering handbills on foot. One day I was on a side street walking up to the house on the corner. I noticed that the front yard of the house had a chain-link fence around it. And as I walked past the side of the house, I quickly discovered why. Inside the fence was a large, snarling dog. The dog snapped and lunged at me from behind the fence as I walked along the fence and turned the corner. I felt certain the dog would tear to me to shreds if it weren't for the fence that stood between us.

Because I wasn't about to go inside that fence, I decided that I would just leave the handbill in the front gate of the fence and then move on to the next house. But when I reached the front gate, my heart stood still. Someone had left the gate open! I stood there frozen in terror as I waited to be shredded by the dog. But then the dog also discovered that the front gate was open. He stopped dead in his tracks and looked at me for a few seconds. He then suddenly started yelping and trying to scoot backward as fast as he could. In his rush to get away, he fell over and then started yowling at the top of his lungs. If someone had been home, I'm sure that person would have thought I was torturing the dog.

The scenario was so comical I couldn't help laughing. "The classic bully!" I thought to myself. He was so brave and ferocious as long as there was a fence between us, but as soon as he had to stand up to me face to face, he was a whimpering coward.

Victims No Longer

In many cases, the victims of bullying don't have the means to stand up to the bullies because the disparity of power between the two parties is too great. But today, kingdom Christians aren't in that situation. We *can* stand up to theological bullies.

When the ferocious dog I encountered was unmasked, I discovered that there was nothing to him. He was all bluff. The same is true of theologians. When we have the courage to unmask the great theological "heroes of the faith," we usually find that they are men who have corrupted the faith. Likewise, when we unmask the learned theologians of today, we usually find that they actually are incompetent phonies.

Let me give you some examples of the incredible incompetence and blindness of today's theologians.

19

Exposing the Blindness of Theologians

When Christians today want help understanding or expounding a passage of Scripture, they typically turn to commentaries, study Bibles, and other works that profess to give insights into what the Bible writers were saying.

But what qualifies such writers to know what Jesus and the apostles "really meant"? Typically, they claim expertise because they have advanced degrees in theology or in some biblical subject. In other words, they are part of the "wise and learned" class—the very class from whom Jesus said the kingdom was hidden.

Bible commentators use three primary methods to give the impression that they have hidden insights into the "real" meaning of the Bible writer: (1) their understanding of Greek, (2) their knowledge of history during the New Testament era, and (3) their familiarity with the historic faith. Yet, in all three of these areas, they repeatedly demonstrate their blindness. In this chapter, let me show you the blindness of many theologians when it comes to Greek.

The Myth of the Greek Language

Anyone reading Bible study materials or listening to typical sermons comes away with the impression that ancient Greek is a "super language" far more precise than English and full of richness that just can't be expressed adequately in English. But just the opposite is true. It's far easier to communicate with precision in modern English than it is with ancient Greek (or any other ancient language).

One reason for this is that the number of ancient Greek words is only three percent or less than that of modern English. Ancient Greek consisted of only 20,000 words. In contrast, the *Oxford English Dictionary* contains about 600,000 words. Yet, even that doesn't come close to including all of the English words used in common speech and writing. Some lexicographers say that English now has more than a million unique words.[1] No other language in human history has had the rich vocabulary of contemporary English.

It makes me think of the situation I faced in art class in grade school. Our family was always on a tight budget, so the new box of crayons my parents bought me at the start of each new school year was the basic Crayola set containing 12 colors. It was certainly sufficient for drawing the pictures I made during art class. However, some of my classmates had the Crayola set with 32 colors, and some even had Crayola's 64-color set.

When it came to blue, my box of crayons had one choice—blue. However, my classmates with the 64-crayon set had not only blue, but also sky blue, dark blue, cornflower, Prussian blue, and others. They could express many varieties of blue in their drawings, whereas I was limited to one color.

It's pretty much the same situation when ancient Greek is compared to contemporary English. To be sure, ancient Greek is more precise than most other ancient languages, such as Hebrew. But it just doesn't match up to a modern language such as English. The issue with New Testament Greek isn't that it's so much more precise than English, but that it's often so much more ambiguous.

For example, take the Greek word *angelos.* It has the basic meaning of "messenger." Yet, as used by the Jews and Christians, the word also can mean "angel." Normally we can tell from the context whether the word should be translated as "messenger" or "angel." But sometimes the context doesn't make it clear, and even the early Christians didn't know for certain whether the Bible writer was talking about angels or human messengers.

For instance, each of the letters to the seven churches in Revelation is addressed to the *angelos* of that church. Does that mean every church has a heavenly angel assigned to it? Or were the letters addressed to the earthly "messenger" of the church—the pastor, presiding elder, or some other person who acted as the spokesman for the church? We simply don't know.

Another example is the Greek word *martyr.* The basic meaning of the word is "witness." But, not surprisingly, the word also means "martyr." Sometimes we can tell from the context how the New

Testament writer is using the term. However, at other times, we simply don't know.

Let me give you another case in point: the Greek word *diatheke*. As used in the New Testament, this word normally means "covenant." For example, Hebrews 8:8 states, "Behold the days are coming, says the Lord, when I will make a new covenant (*diatheke*) with the house of Israel and with the house of Judah." Yet in the next chapter, the same writer says, "For where there is a testament (*diatheke*), there must also of necessity be the death of the testator. For a testament (*diatheke*) is in force after men are dead, since it has no power at all while the testator lives" (Heb. 9:16,17).

The Greek word *diatheke* is used 21 times in Hebrews. In 19 of those instances, the word means covenant. Yet in the passage quoted above, it obviously means a Last Will and Testament. A covenant or contract doesn't require the death of the party making the contract. But a Last Will and Testament does. It is not a covenant that "has no power at all while the testator lives." It is a Last Will and Testament that has no power while the testator lives. The issue isn't the richness of the Greek word *diatheke*, but its ambiguity. Whereas English has different words for covenant and testament, *koiné* Greek had only one word for both items.

The problem isn't that most Greek words had more than one meaning. Most English words have more than one meaning, too. But in English we normally have a list of synonyms from which we can choose to make our meaning clear. In ancient Greek, there often was only one word available—with all its ambiguity.

Furthermore, ancient Greek was written without any punctuation. There were no commas, periods, parentheses, or quotation marks. Imagine trying to write a letter or document today without any punctuation. It's not hard to imagine the confusion that would result. In comparing different New Testament translations, I've noticed that translators don't always agree on where to place commas and where to end and begin sentences. That's not the fault of the translators; it's the limitation of ancient Greek.

Please don't think that I'm denigrating Greek scholars. I'm very grateful to the translators who have given us the Bible in English and to the scholars who've published Greek-English dictionaries and interlinear Bibles. We're all deeply indebted to them. My knowledge of Greek is miniscule compared with theirs.

The situation is similar to that of medical doctors. Their knowledge of the human body and of disease is vastly superior to my own. Yet, that doesn't mean that I just have to accept without question everything my doctor says. In fact, I've found that most competent doctors don't object to my disputing their diagnosis occasionally, if I do so in a respectful manner. I've found that the doctors usually are right, but on several occasions my dissenting opinion proved to be correct.

Greek scholars are normally right, but their opinions shouldn't be accepted without question. Furthermore, I've found that it's usually not the real Greek scholars who pretend ancient Greek is some magical language that means all sorts of things that ordinary English can't express. It's the commentators and other theologians who've had a few years of Greek in divinity school and who use their limited knowledge of Greek to bully others.

The Foolishness of Root Meanings

I'm sure we've all listened to sermons during which the speaker reads a passage of Scripture and then says, "Now, the Greek here literally means . . ." The speaker then uses the "literal meaning" to re-interpret the passage, making it say something different from what we read in our Bibles. The problem with this approach is that the speaker is not really stating what the word or passage *literally* means. Instead, he's merely giving the etymology of the word—that is, its root meaning.

The folly of this approach is that the root meaning of a word usually has little bearing on what that word actually means in the time and circumstances in which it is written. We all instinctively know that this is true with English.

For example, in Texas there's an immense amount of oil and gas production. As a result, when landowners sell their property, they typically reserve the "oil and gas" so that they can continue to own the petroleum after the property is sold. Now, let's suppose that John Doe sold his property to Bob Smith, reserving the "oil and gas." Let's further suppose that Bob Smith planted a grove of olive trees on his land. When it comes time to harvest the olives, John Doe comes driving up in his pickup and tells Bob not to harvest the olives, because they belong to him.

"What?" Bob would no doubt say in disbelief. "What makes you think you own the olives?"

"Because I reserved the oil and gas on this property. And the literal meaning of *oil* is 'olive.' Therefore, I'm entitled to all the olives."

If the matter went to court, what do you think the court would do? No doubt, John would be laughed out of court. The fact that *olive* is the root meaning of *oil* has absolutely no bearing on what the word means in ordinary usage today. In Texas, when sellers reserve the oil under their land, everyone understands that they are reserving the petroleum.

We all can see how ludicrous it would be in English to try to interpret a document based on the etymologies or root meanings of the words used. What is farcical in English doesn't somehow become logical and insightful when we switch to Greek. My dictionary defines "literal" as "based on the actual words in their ordinary meaning; not figurative or symbolic."[2] So the *literal* meaning of a word is not its root origin, but its normal meaning in context at the time it is written or spoken.

Let's face it, most people don't even know the root origins of the words they use. I certainly don't. Did you know that our word *gas* comes from the Greek word meaning "chaos"? I didn't. I was also surprised to learn that the root word for *employee* means "to fold," and that the root meaning of *coin* is "wedge." I could go on and on. Word meanings typically undergo numerous changes over time. So the root meaning of a word is irrelevant when interpreting any written instrument. It might make an interesting piece of trivia, but nothing more.

Yet, commentators and theologians continue to use word etymologies as a means to interpret Scripture. It is ignorant, dishonest, and blind—but they continue to get away with it.

How Do We Know What a Word Means?

All of this raises the question: How does anybody know what an ancient Greek word meant in the first century? The issue is neither what a particular Greek word means *today* nor its root meaning. The question is: What did it mean to the New Testament writers and their readers?

It's important to understand that there were no Greek dictionaries written in ancient times, nor do we have any ancient Greek grammar textbooks. So to arrive at the proper meaning of a New Testament word, we have to examine how that word was used in ancient sources. With regard to the New Testament, we have three main sources:

- Classical Greek texts
- The Septuagint (the ancient Greek translation of the Old Testament)
- The early Christian writings, particularly those of the second century.

The beginning place for the study of ancient Greek has generally been the Greek classics, of which there are many. There are some limitations on this, however. For one thing, the New Testament was written in the common *koiné* Greek—not the polished Greek of the classics. Second, most of the classic Greek works were written many centuries before the New Testament. Like any other language, the meaning of Greek words changed over time. So what a Greek word meant in the time of Plato (c. 400 B.C.) is not necessarily what it meant in the days of the apostles. Finally, the biblical writers often used words in a different sense than the secular writers.

So for the study of New Testament Greek, the Septuagint is a far more valuable resource than the classics. For one thing, it was written in *koiné* Greek. Second, it was much closer in time to the New Testament than the writings of philosophers such as Plato and Aristotle. Finally, the Septuagint was *the* Old Testament of the first-century church. Both the apostles and their readers were steeped in the vocabulary of the Septuagint, and this is reflected in the vocabulary of the New Testament. As one Greek scholar noted: "Humanly speaking, without the Septuagint, there could have been no New Testament. For the Septuagint provided to the New Testament not only its vehicle of language, but also to a great extent its patterns of thought."[3]

Despite this, I find that most New Testament commentators and theologians are abysmally ignorant about the Septuagint. My guess is that most of them have never read it.

The writings of the early Christians—particularly those in the first century after the close of the New Testament—are another extremely valuable resource. The Christians of that age spoke the same language, lived in the same culture, and used the same Christian vocabulary as the apostles. When looking into the meaning of a New Testament Greek word, a key question should always be: How did the first- and second-century Christians understand the apostles' words? That's only common sense. Yet, once again, I find that most commentators and Bible expositors are totally ignorant of how the early Christians understood the New Testament.

As I've mentioned, I'm no Greek scholar. My special field of study has been Christian history— particularly early Christian history. But as a historian, I can't help but notice that the early Christians were obviously understanding certain New Testament words and sentences differently from what our "experts" today tell us those words and sentences mean.

Agape: A Case in Point

Like most of you, I grew up being taught that *agape*, one of the Greek words for love used in the New Testament, has a special meaning that differentiates it from other Greek words for love, such as *eros* or *philia*. We've all heard that *agape* love is the highest form of love, that it is unconditional love, or that it means seeking the highest good of another person. In contrast, we're told that *philia* is merely having affection for someone or liking that person. Finally, we're told that *eros* is romantic love. One Christian source puts it this way:

> *Philia* is an emotional, brotherly love, a love which would best be illustrated in the Bible as that between David and Jonathan. It is important that the command to love is never *phileo*, because it is an emotional love that comes out of a mutual reciprocal relationship, but rather *agape*. . . .
>
> Finally there is the Greek word for love: *agape*, which represents an attitude of love that is non-selfish. It has a selfless interest with its focus on primar-

ily giving to others. Agape can be described as unconditional positive regard, a personal state of mind that spurs us into helpful, needful action in personal simplicity, humility, compassion and equanimity. Agape is the higher form, a manifestation of God's true love for all of us which we all still do need to personally have, promote, cultivate by letting God have full control of our lives.

The Greek word *agape* is mostly foreign to classical Greek because it's origin is from God. (1 Jn. 4:7—for love comes from God). The first disciples of Jesus Christ were incapable of agape love until after Pentecost, for agape love comes from the Holy Spirit alone."[4]

I've heard this type of teaching most of my life and have even said similar things myself in sermons. Therefore, you can imagine my surprise when I read the early Christian writings and noticed that they never said there was anything special about the word *agape*. That got me to wondering.

So I checked to see if the word *agape* appears anywhere in the Septuagint. In other words, was it a Greek word primarily used only by Christians? Or did the Jews use the word a century or more before the time of Christ? To my surprise, I found that *agape* is used 283 times in the Septuagint, from Genesis through Malachi. So it's not true that it was a special word virtually unknown before our New Testament. The reason Jesus and His apostles used *agape* so often is because it's the word the Greek-speaking Jews were accustomed to reading in the Old Testament.

Obviously it's not true that humans were incapable of agape love before Pentecost. After all, in the

Septuagint, God commanded the Israelites to "love (*agape*) the Lord your God with all your heart, with all your soul, and with all your strength" (Deut. 6:5). The Septuagint also uses *agape* in the commandment to love one's neighbor as oneself. Was God commanding the Israelites to do something they were incapable of doing before Pentecost? Obviously not, for the Old Testament speaks of persons who loved God. (Ps. 5:11; 18:1; 31:23; 97:10; 119:127). In each of those places, the Septuagint uses *agape*.

What about the claim that the type of friendship love that David and Jonathan had for each other was *philia*, not *agape*? False again! In describing David's reaction on hearing about Jonathan's death, the Septuagint reads, "I am grieved for you, my brother Jonathan; you were most pleasant to me. Your love (*agape*) for me was to be admired, surpassing the love (*agape*) of women" (2 Sa. 1:26).[5]

What about the claim that agape love is a higher, selfless love that can be produced only by the Holy Spirit? Once again, false! In reading the Septuagint, I found that the Jews used *agape* to cover all forms of love: love of God, affection for friends, romantic love, and even love of wrong things. Here are a few examples of the many ways that *agape* love is used in the Greek version of the Old Testament:

"Then make me savory food, such as I *love*, and bring it to me that I may eat." (Gn. 27:4).

"How long, O you sons of men, will you turn my glory to shame? How long will you *love* worthlessness? (Ps. 4:2).

"Those who hate me *love* death" (Pr. 8:36).

"Your *love* is better than wine, and the smell of your ointments is better than all spices. . . . The young maidens *love* you. . . . I sought him whom my soul *loves*; I sought him, but did not find him. . . . Much water will not be able to quench *love*, nor will rivers drown it" (Song 1:2,3; 3:1; 8:7).

Thoroughly intrigued from discovering these things, I decided to search the New Testament to see how the word *agape* is used there. Consistent with the Septuagint, I found that Jesus and the apostles used *agape* to cover various types of love. In each of the passages below, the Greek word used for love is *agape*:

"Even sinners *love* those who *love* them" (Lk. 6:32).

"Woe to you Pharisees! For you *love* the best seats in the synagogues and greetings in the marketplaces" (Lk. 11:43).

"Men *loved* darkness rather than light, because their deeds were evil" (Jn. 3:19).

"They *loved* the praise of men more than the praise of God" (Jn. 12:43).

"Demas has forsaken me, having *loved* this present world" (2 Ti. 4:10).

"They have forsaken the right way and gone astray, following the way of Balaam the son of Beor, who *loved* the wages of unrighteousness" (2 Pe. 2:15).

"Do not *love* the world or the things in the world" (1 Jn. 2:15).

Well, so much for our learned commentators!

Yet, if theologians and commentators are often blind guides when it comes to the Greek language, they are infinitely more so when it comes to New Testament history.

20

Counterfeit History

When I was in my early thirties, about the only Christian works I read besides the Scriptures were commentaries and similar reference works. I believed practically every word that commentators wrote. They seemed to know so much about what was happening "behind the scenes" in the New Testament church. It seemed there had to be an abundance of Jewish and Christian writings from the first century that shed tremendous light on the Bible.

Eventually, I decided to read those same writings for myself, instead of always having to rely on others for this information. So I eagerly began digging to see where I could purchase some of these first-century writings that revealed so much about what was happening in the New Testament churches. And that's when I discovered the Big Secret!

The Big Secret

The big secret is that such first-century writings that reveal so much about first-century Judaism and Christianity simply *don't exist*. I was utterly shocked when I discovered this. The commentators seem to know so much about what was happening behind the scenes in the apostolic age. Surely they don't make all of that up! But, yes indeed, that is the very thing that they do.

Let me give you some examples of what I'm talking about. John Calvin invented this "behind the scenes" look at what was happening in the first-century church:

> A conjecture is drawn, with some appearance of probability, that women who had beautiful hair were accustomed to uncover their heads for the purpose of showing off their beauty. It is not, therefore, without good reason that Paul, as a remedy for this vice, sets before them the opposite idea—that they be regarded as remarkable for unseemliness, rather than for what is an incentive to lust.[1]

So according to Calvin, the Corinthian sisters were uncovering their heads to show off their beautiful hair. At least Calvin admits that this is a conjecture.

But William Burkitt, a popular commentator of the early 1700s, provides a very different "inside story" of what was happening in Corinth:

> [This was] a fantastical imitation of the she-priests and prophetesses of the Gentiles when they served their idols, and particularly when they sacrificed to Bacchus, who used to have their faces uncovered, their hair disheveled, hanging at its full length round about their ears.
>
> Now the Corinthian women, in imitation of these heathen women, (for the female sex is very fond and exceeding prone to follow the fashion) cast off their veils, uncovered their faces, and dishonored their heads.[2]

So now we're told that the problem in Corinth was that the Christian women were wanting to imitate the pagan prophetesses. This time, do we have the "real story"? Not according to the famous commentators, Jamieson, Fausset, and Brown. In their commentary published in 1871 they give us a different "inside story":

> The Corinthian women, on the ground of the abolition of distinction of sexes in Christ, claimed equality with the male sex, and, overstepping the bounds of propriety, came forward to pray and prophesy without the customary head-covering of females.[3]

So now we're told that what was really happening in Corinth was that the women were claiming social equality with men. Other commentators quickly adopted this view. For example, the 1942 work entitled *Commentary on the Whole Bible* repeats this claim:

> Now St. Paul himself taught that 'there can be no male and female; for ye are all one in Christ Jesus' (Galatians 3, written either shortly before or shortly after 1 Corinthians). By this he meant that salvation is offered to all alike, all are alike in spiritual position; but these women had taken such teaching to mean that all social subordination to men was all done away.[4]

So first the problem was that the Corinthian women wanted to show off their beautiful hair. Then the problem was that the sisters at Corinth were wanting to imitate the pagan prophetesses. Next the problem was that the Corinthian sisters were early feminists claiming the same authoritative rights in the congregation as men. Somehow the "real story" keeps changing.

But that's not surprising. As I said, my experience has been that the "background history" given by commentators is nearly always made up. After all, how can someone living nearly two thousand years later in a different part of the world possibly know what was going on in the first-century Corinthian church? The passage in 1 Corinthians 11 tells us nothing whatsoever about why Paul had to remind the Corinthians of the church-wide practice. I think we can reasonably infer that either men were praying with covered heads, or women were praying with uncovered heads—or both. But that's the most the passage itself reveals.

The commentators give the impression that they have access to some additional Christian writings from the time of Paul that reveal what really was going on. But no such writings exist. There is nothing. *Nada!*

The only helpful Christian writings we have are those of the early church, written after the deaths of the apostles. What we learn from their writings is that the New Testament commandment on the head covering was practiced throughout the entire Christian world, in all countries and cultures.[5] It wasn't something peculiar to Corinth. Second, we learn that the head covering was some type of *cloth* covering, the style of which differed among various cultures.[6] The covering was not long hair, as some persons have tried to argue in modern times.

However, the early Christian writers don't purport to know what the background events had been in the first-century Corinthian church—even though such writers lived only a century or so later.

Yet, our modern commentators, living nearly two thousand years later, profess to know exactly what was going on in the first-century Corinthian church!

Writings of the Rabbis

A new trend in modern times is to create background information for the New Testament by referring to things said in "rabbinical literature." Modern commentators give the impression that they have a wealth of inside knowledge on what the rabbis were teaching in Jesus' day, and that this knowledge throws a significant light on Jesus' teachings and actions.

But the truth of the matter is that no such writings exist from the first century. We do have a handful of Jewish writings from the first century, but they are not rabbinical writings—and they shed little light on Jesus' teaching. The three primary Jewish sources we have from the first century are Josephus, Philo, and the sectarian writings of the Essenes.

Josephus

Josephus was a first-century Jewish historian who provides us with valuable historical information about the Jewish political scene in the first century and the centuries immediately preceding it. He tells us about the Jewish war with Rome and the destruction of Jerusalem in A.D. 70. He also gives a brief description of the Pharisees, Sadducees, and Essenes. Finally, he tells about the martyrdom of James, the brother of Jesus.

All information is extremely valuable. However, there is nothing in Josephus that tells anything about church life in the first century or about the teachings of the rabbis. The "behind the scenes" Jewish information in the commentaries doesn't come from Josephus.

Philo

Philo was an Alexandrian Jew who lived at the same time as Jesus, although their two paths never crossed. Philo was a well-educated man highly respected in the Jewish community at Alexandria. But he also was a thoroughly Hellenized Jew. In his writings, he interprets much of the Old Testament allegorically to make it better fit with Greek thought. As far as shedding any light on the New Testament, his writings are essentially worthless.

The Qumran Community

The sectarian writings of the Qumran community, which have been found among the Dead Sea Scrolls, are of even less help than Josephus and Philo. That's because the Qumran sectarians—who were probably Essenes—had separated themselves from normal Jewish life and had created an isolated commune in the region of the Dead Sea. Their writings consist primarily of apocalyptic works and specialized rules for their community. To our knowledge, neither Jesus nor His apostles had any interaction with these people.

There Must Be Some Mistake!

I can't blame you if you're thinking to yourself, "David, surely you're mistaken about this. There have to be a lot more relevant first-century Jewish writings than that. After all, there's all the rabbinical writings to which the commentators keep referring."

Well, you don't have to take my word for it. Go and diligently search for these missing writings. See for yourself if you can find any relevant Jewish first-century writings beyond the three I've mentioned.

But what about the Jewish rabbinical writings we hear so much about? The truth is that we have no rabbinical writings from the first century. The earliest rabbinical writings we have are contained in the Mishnah. But it was not written in the first century. Rather, it dates from the beginning of the third century. The Mishnah is a collection of various rabbinical interpretations of specific commandments in the Law, such as the Sabbath. It includes interpretations that were purportedly handed down orally from scribes who lived in the first century.

The examples I used at the beginning of this book about how the scribes interpreted the Law come from the Mishnah. We don't know for certain that those specific interpretations were being taught in Jesus' day, but they fit the description Jesus gave of the scribes' teaching. That is, they strained out the gnat and swallowed the camel. The Mishnah also reveals that the rabbis had conflicting teachings and interpretations on almost every area of the Law. In the third century A.D., a supplement to the Mishnah was compiled, known as the Tosefta. It is very similar in form to the Mishnah.

Although the Mishnah and Tosefta are available today, surprisingly, the so-called "inside information" we find in commentaries rarely, if ever, comes from the Mishnah or Tosefta.

The Talmud

The major influential rabbinical work of all time is the Talmud.* However, it was not written down until about A.D. 500. The Talmud consists of the Mishnah plus all of the rabbinical commentary on the Mishnah made between the years A.D. 200 through 500. So the Talmud is of little value in shedding any light on the beliefs and practices of Jews in the first century. It's only a record of rabbinical discussions and teachings as they were remembered 400 years after the close of the New Testament.

It would be quite dishonest for commentators to quote the Talmud as though it represents Jewish beliefs and practices in the first century. For it reflects rabbinical thought centuries after the New Testament was written. And like the Mishnah, the Talmud contains contradictory opinions between various rabbis.

Yet, once again, the supposed "Jewish inside information" of Christian commentators is rarely even based on something in the Talmud. It's either something the commentators snatched from a medieval rabbinical source, such as a prayer book or—in most cases—it's something they've made up. Commentators make up things not only about Jewish beliefs and practices, but about Roman and Greek practices as well.

I realize that what I'm saying may be hard to believe, so let me give you a few examples.

---

* Actually, there are two Talmuds: the Jerusalem and the Babylonian. And the two often say different things. Of the two, the Babylonian Talmud has been the most influential.

21

When Fiction Is Presented as Fact

Perhaps no passage in Scripture has had as much counterfeit history written about it as the passage we've been discussing in 1 Corinthians 11 about the head covering. As we've already discussed, commentators act as if they know what was happening behind the scenes within the Corinthian church. In truth, none of us know anything.

Theologians also pretend to have many insights about the pagan world in which those Corinthian Christians lived. For example, the nineteenth-century commentator, Adam Clarke, says this about that passage:

> The only difference marked by the apostle was, the man had his head uncovered, because he was the representative of Christ; the woman had hers covered, because she was placed by the order of God in a state of subjection to the man, *and* because it was a custom, both among the Greeks and Romans, and among the Jews an express law, that no woman should be seen abroad without a veil. This was, and is, a common custom through all the east, and none but public prostitutes go without veils.[1] (italics mine)

A person doesn't have to read any further than his own Bible to be able to spot Clarke's first fabrication. He indicates that the apostle required a woman to have her head covered when praying and prophesying "because she was placed by the order of God in a state of subjection to the man, <u>and</u> because it was a custom, both among the Greeks and Romans, and among the Jews an express law, that no woman should be seen abroad without a veil."

However, what Paul said was: "Every woman who prays or prophesies with her head uncovered dishonors her head, for that is one and the same as if her head were shaved. For if a woman is not covered, let her also be shorn. But if it is shameful for a woman to be shorn or shaved, let her be covered. For a man indeed ought not to cover his head, since he is the image and glory of God; but woman is the glory of man. For man is not from woman, but woman from man. Nor was man created for the woman, but woman for the man. For this reason the woman ought to have a symbol of authority on her head, because of the angels" (1 Cor. 11:5–10).

Now Paul gives two reasons for his instructions: (1) headship and (2) "because of the angels." Nowhere does he say anything about Roman, Greek, or Jewish customs. That's something that Adam Clarke made up. Unfortunately, that wasn't Clarke's only fabrication. Let's look at some of his others.

Greek and Roman Customs

Clarke claims that it was a Greek and Roman custom that "no woman should be seen abroad without a veil." But, as is true with most commentators,

Clarke offers no proof for this assertion. I'm certainly no authority on Greek or Roman public life, but I have read many ancient Greek and Roman writings. And I've never come across anything indicating that Greek and Roman women were not to appear in public without veils. I also have seen plenty of Greek and Roman sculptures and paintings from the New Testament era. And they certainly don't validate Clarke's assertion either.

What we do learn from Greek and Roman literature and art is that in the New Testament era some Roman and Greek women wore transparent veils at various times. Such veils appear to have been worn more for adornment than anything else. We also know that Greek and Roman women typically wore a shawl, known as a *palla*, around their shoulders. Sometimes they draped this over their heads. However, there's certainly nothing in Greek and Roman literature to connect the *palla* with any teaching on headship.

Jewish Women and the Veil

Next, Clarke boldly proclaims that among the Jews it was an "express law that no woman should be seen abroad without a veil." But the only "express law" the first-century Jews had was the Mosaic Law. And any Christian can read the Law and see that there is no such commandment in the Law.

"Yes, but perhaps the rabbis had made some additional law about the veil," you may reply. But, as I've mentioned, we don't have any rabbinical writings from the New Testament period. The earliest collection of rabbinical teachings we have is the

Mishnah (c. 200 A.D.), and there is nothing in the Mishnah that requires a Jewish woman to wear a veil when she goes out in public.

In fact, I've been able to find only one brief reference to the veil in the Mishnah. It's in the section that discusses what men and women may wear in public on the Sabbath. It says this: "A woman may go out in hair ribbons . . . and with a headband, sewn head bangles, a hairnet, or false locks. . . . Arabian women may go out veiled. Median women may go out with cloaks looped up over their shoulders."[2]

So there was certainly no express law in the Mishnah that women *had* to wear a veil. Actually, the Mishnah forbids a woman to wear a veil on the Sabbath unless she resides in Arabia—where all women were expected to wear a veil in public. This would indicate that the Jewish veil was worn primarily for adornment. That's the very thing we see in Scripture. Isaiah prophesied concerning the Israelite women:

> Because the daughters of Zion are haughty, and walk with outstretched necks and wanton eyes, walking and mincing as they go, making a jingling with their feet, therefore the Lord will strike with a scab the crown of the head of the daughters of Zion, and the Lord will uncover their secret parts. In that day the Lord will take away the finery: the jingling anklets, the scarves, and the crescents; the pendants, the bracelets, and the veils; the headdresses, the leg ornaments, and the headbands; the perfume boxes, the charms, and the rings (Is. 3:16–21).

So evidently the veil was customarily worn by Jewish women. But it was an ornament, not a symbol of headship.

Actually, one of the most revealing sources of evidence we have about Jewish women and the veil is found in a work of the early Christian writer, Tertullian. He says, "Among the Jews, so usual is it for their women to have the head veiled, that they may thereby be recognized."[3] This is a significant piece of historical evidence. It not only verifies that Jewish women customarily wore veils (as the Scriptures indicate), but it also reveals that most Gentile women in Tertullian's day *didn't*. If a Jewish woman could be recognized because she wore a veil, then obviously the Roman women weren't normally wearing them. And the Christians that Paul wrote to in Corinth were primarily Greeks and Romans—not Jews.

An Eastern Custom?

Next, Clarke claims that veiling "was, and is, a common custom through all the east." What Clarke said is similar to what Matthew Henry said in his commentary concerning this passage: "To understand this, it must be observed that it was a signification either of shame or subjection for persons to be veiled, or covered, in the eastern countries."[4] Most commentaries today say similar things.

But are their claims true? To begin with, it's not true that the veil was symbolic of "shame or subjection," as Matthew Henry claims. It's just the contrary. As we've seen, Isaiah shows that the veil was a symbol of pride and ornament for Jewish women.

That's why the Mishnah forbids women from wearing a veil on the Sabbath.

Of course, most people today know that it's customary today in the Mideast for women to wear a veil or scarf. So most Christians accept without question that eastern women wore veils in Paul's day. Ah, but is that true? You see, women wear veils in most Middle Eastern countries today because those are Muslim countries. But Islam didn't even come into existence until the seventh century A.D.—hundreds of years after the New Testament was written. Islam exported Arabian culture to the countries it conquered. And as I've mentioned, Arabian women customarily wore veils in ancient times.[5]

The question is not "What do women in the Middle East wear *today*?" but "What were the dress customs in the Middle East in *Paul's* day, before Islam?" In other words, how did Egyptians, Syrians, Galatians, Persians, Chaldeans, Elamites, and other peoples of the Middle East dress in the first century? That is no easy task to discover. It's not as though there were any encyclopedias, picture books, or travelogues from that time.

Nevertheless, we do have paintings, statues, and artifacts from ancient Egypt, Syria, Persia, Assyria, and Babylonia. You've no doubt seen pictures of ancient Egyptian women found in tombs and other places. The Egyptian women in those paintings normally don't have their heads covered, do they? In some Middle Eastern countries, such as Syria, the paintings and statues would indicate that women commonly wore shawls that they could drape over their heads. However, in other places, the paintings and sculptures indicate that the women wore no kind of head covering at all—the same as in ancient Egypt.[6]

To read the customs of Mideastern countries today back into Paul's day is the mark of a blind guide. But the blindness of theologians and commentators goes even further in this regard. Even a child can look at a world atlas and see that Corinth is not situated in the East. It's located in Greece, and Greece is known as the "cradle of *western* civilization." Ancient Corinth was not an eastern city. So, in the end, even if all of the commentators' remarks about eastern civilization were accurate, they're completely irrelevant.

Prostitutes and Corinth

Adam Clarke's final claim—one often repeated today—is that only prostitutes went around in public without a veil. Nowadays, most commentators, such as William Barclay, claim that Corinth was a licentious city filled with prostitutes. The commentators say that it was important for the Christian women to wear veils so they wouldn't be mistaken for prostitutes.

To begin with, Paul says nothing about any such thing as the reason for the head covering. The only reasons he gives are headship and "because of the angels." Furthermore, commentators all seem to forget that the head covering is a two-part commandment: one for men and one for women. If the issue was prostitutes, why would Paul tell *men* to uncover their heads when praying or prophesying? What are the commentators going to tell us next—

that the only men in Corinth who covered their heads were male prostitutes?

What's more, these commentators are somehow mistakenly interpreting 1 Corinthians 11 as though the head covering was a special commandment given only to the Corinthians. However, the force of Paul's argument is that apparently some of the Corinthians weren't following the practice already in place in the *rest* of the church. The commandment has nothing to do with Corinth. The only reason the commandment is found in Paul's letter to the Corinthians is that apparently some in the Corinthian church were rebelling against it.

Furthermore, where is the evidence that only prostitutes went out in public without a veil?* As we've already seen from Tertullian's earlier quotation, Jewish women were recognizable because they wore a veil. So obviously, most Greek and Roman women in his day didn't wear a veil. So it's untrue that only prostitutes didn't wear veils. This is merely another piece of pseudo history fabricated by commentators. There's a reason why none of them ever provide any historical evidence to back up their claims. It's because there is no such evidence.

---

* When commentators say that the only women who didn't wear veils in ancient times were prostitutes, I have to wonder if they've ever read the account in Genesis about Tamar. When she wanted to appear to be a prostitute, she didn't *take off* her veil. Instead, she put one on. The account says, "So she took off her widow's garments, covered herself with a veil and wrapped herself, and sat in an open place which was on the way to Timnah. . . . When Judah saw her, he thought she was a harlot, because she had covered her face" (Gn. 38:14, 15). So some prostitutes did wear veils in ancient times.

Finally, what about this business of Corinth being a particularly licentious city filled with prostitutes? In his commentary, Barclay calls it "probably the most licentious city in the world."[7] The rumor that Corinth was exceptionally licentious probably got started from a passage found in the ancient work, *Geography,* written by the Roman geographer, Strabo. In his work, Strabo says this about Corinth:

> And the temple of Aphrodite was so rich that it owned more than a thousand temple slaves, prostitutes, whom both men and women had dedicated to the goddess. And therefore it was also on account of these women that the city was crowded with people and grew rich. For instance, the ship captains freely squandered their money, and hence the proverb, "Not for every man is the voyage to Corinth."[8]

Well, at first glance, it seems that the Roman geographer Strabo confirms that the commentators are at least correct in saying that Corinth was a licentious city. Perhaps the commentators finally have some of their history correct! Or do they? Let's keep reading what Strabo has to say:

> The Corinthians, when they were subject to Philip, not only sided with him in his quarrel with the Romans, but individually behaved so contemptuously towards the Romans that certain persons ventured to pour down filth upon the Roman ambassadors when passing by their house. However, for this and other offenses, they soon paid the penalty. For a considerable army was sent there, and the city itself was razed to the ground. . . .
>
> Now after Corinth had remained deserted for a long time, it was rebuilt by the deified Caesar because of its favorable position. He colonized it with people

that belonged for the most part to the freedmen class.[9]

So the truth is that the Greek Corinth with its temple to Aphrodite and a thousand prostitutes was completely destroyed, and the site remained desolate for a long time. In 44 B. C., Julius Caesar rebuilt a new Corinth. This new Corinth had no temple to Aphrodite, and it was a Roman colony—meaning that Roman citizens (in this case, freedmen) settled there. So the Corinth that existed in Paul's day was the Roman Corinth, which had no special reputation for prostitutes or immorality. In fact, Strabo concludes his discussion about Roman Corinth by saying:

> The city of the Corinthians, then, was always great and wealthy, and it was well equipped with men skilled both in the affairs of state and in the craftsman's arts. For both here and in Sicyon the arts of painting and sculpturing and all such arts of the craftsman flourished the most. However, the city had land that was not very fertile, but rifted and rough. And from this fact, everyone calls Corinth "protruding," and they use the proverb, "Corinth is both protruding and full of hollows."[10]

So by Paul's day, Corinth was no longer known for its prostitutes, but for its skilled craftsmen and infertile land.

Now, what I've given you is merely one example of the counterfeit history that theologians use to distort what the Scriptures actually teach. I could fill volumes with examples of the counterfeit history found in commentaries, study Bibles, and other theological literature. Let me give you a few more examples.

22

Men Didn't Talk to Women—And Other Lies

U
nfortunately, rather than diminishing, the pseudo history of the theologians has only proliferated in the past few decades. Yet, often Christians have to go no further than their own Bibles to expose these historical myths. Let me share three such examples with you.

Men Didn't Talk to Women?

One of the most absurd claims being made today is that Jewish men disdained women and therefore refused to talk to them. This claim is usually made when commentators discuss Jesus' encounter with the Samaritan woman, described in the fourth chapter of John. While His disciples were buying food in a nearby city, Jesus conversed with a woman at a well. When His disciples returned, the Scriptures say, "They marveled that He talked with a woman" (Jn. 4:27).

"Aha!" our theologians tell us. "See. Men in Jesus' day looked down on women and refused to talk to them in public." So, according to modern commentators, Jesus was doing something revolutionary merely by talking to a woman. They then argue that it was Jesus who started the feminist movement.

But what do the facts show? Taken out of context, that sentence—"they marveled that He talked with a woman"—sounds as though men didn't speak to women in Jesus' day. However, when we read the entire passage, we immediately see that this wasn't the issue at all.

The context is that Jesus and His disciples were passing through Samaria. While the disciples were purchasing food at the nearby town of Sychar, Jesus waited outside the city by a well. When a Samaritan woman came to the well to fetch water, Jesus asked her for a drink. The Samaritan woman was surprised that Jesus talked to her.

But why was the woman surprised? Because Jewish men didn't speak to women? Not at all. The Scripture tells us exactly why: "Then the woman of Samaria said to Him, 'How is it that You, being a Jew, ask a drink from me, a Samaritan woman? For Jews have no dealings with Samaritans'" (Jn. 4:9). Ah, right there we have the answer. She didn't say, "For men have no dealings with women," but "Jews have no dealings with Samaritans." The unusual thing was not that a man was speaking to a woman, but that a Jew was speaking to a Samaritan.

When the disciples returned from the town, they too were surprised that Jesus was speaking to a Samaritan woman. But it had nothing to do with gender. It had to do with her nationality. This is evident from what followed. When the woman left Jesus, she "went her way into the city, and said to the men, 'Come, see a Man who told me all things that I ever did. Could this be the Christ?'" (Jn. 4:28,29). So the Samaritan woman felt free to converse with the men of the city. There was no gender barrier to such conversation. Did the men brush the woman off in scorn when she spoke to them? Not at all. They went and did exactly what she asked them to do.

Of course, anyone who has read the Bible knows that men spoke with women throughout the Old and New Testaments. Jesus didn't do anything unusual. In Genesis, we have a situation very similar to the Samaritan woman at the well. Abraham's servant rested at a well outside of the city of Nahor. When a young woman came to the well to draw water, he said essentially the same thing that Jesus said to the Samaritan woman: "And the servant ran to meet her and said, 'Please let me drink a little water from your pitcher'" (Gen. 24:17). Now, did this woman draw back and say, "How is it that you, a man, speak to me, a woman?" Of course not. She replied, "Drink, my lord," and she gave the man a drink (Gen. 24:18).

No, there was nothing unusual about men speaking to women. Jacob spoke to Rachel before they were married, the men of Israel came to Deborah the prophetess for judgments, Boaz spoke to Ruth, and Eli spoke to Hannah. (Gen. 29:11,12; Jdg. 4:3–5; Ruth 2:5–11;1 Sa. 1:13–17). A notable incident in the time of David shows that Jewish men viewed women with esteem, not disdain. David's general, Joab, was pursuing a rebel named Sheba, who had fled to the city of Abel. Joab then besieged the city. The Scriptures tell us what happened next:

> Then a wise woman cried out from the city, "Hear, Hear! Please say to Joab, 'Come nearby, that I may speak with you.'"
>
> When he had come near to her, the woman said, "Are you Joab?"
>
> He answered, "I am."
>
> Then she said to him, "Hear the words of your maidservant."
>
> And he answered, "I am listening" (2 Sa. 20:16–22).

The account goes on to relate that Joab explained whom he was seeking, and the woman told Joab that the city would deliver the man's head to Joab. Once they did this, Joab withdrew. So men not only spoke with women, but also listened to their advice when given in wisdom.

Elijah spoke to the widow of Zarephath and even lodged with her.[1] Likewise, Elisha spoke with the widow of one of the sons of the prophets and performed a miracle on her behalf. Obviously, Jesus did nothing revolutionary by speaking to a woman.

"But," you may say, "I've heard it said that the rabbis taught that a man shouldn't even speak to his wife if he happens to see her in public." Yes, I've heard claims like that as well. But have you ever seen anybody produce an actual quotation to that affect? I certainly haven't. I've examined the Mishnah, and it gives no such instructions. I've even checked the Talmud, although it wasn't compiled until nearly 500 years after Christ. And it contains no such statement. There are instructions and restrictions in the Talmud concerning the intermingling of the

sexes. But this has to do with propriety between the sexes, not disdain for women.

Is it possible that some rabbi in the Middle Ages or some later time said something to the effect that men shouldn't speak to women? Of course, it's possible. But what does that have to do with anything? I can produce quotations from Christian bishops from the Middle Ages on all sorts of subjects. Does that mean that any first-century Christians held to those views? Hardly.

Afraid to Say "God"

As you may have guessed, I quit using commentaries and study Bibles many years ago when I discovered that they contain so much misinformation. However, in the course of research for this book, I purchased or borrowed a number of commentaries and study Bibles just to see what they're saying these days. Usually, I only had to read a few pages in these works before I came across either counterfeit history or some other obvious error.

For example, just a few pages into the *New International Bible Commentary on Matthew*, I found this assertion: "Matthew uses the term 'kingdom of heaven' (rather than kingdom of God) out of Semitic reluctance to speak the divine name."[2] In talking about "Semitic reluctance," I assume that the commentator is referring to the fact that Matthew wrote his Gospel with Jewish readers in mind.[3]

Now, it's true that Orthodox Jews *today* never utter the Divine name YHWH and often avoid even saying God.[4] But the commentator has committed the same error made by the various commentators on 1 Corinthians 11. That is, he is assuming we can read a modern or medieval practice back into New Testament times.

I have to say that it would be ironic if Matthew used the phrase "kingdom of heaven" to avoid using the term God. That's because he uses "God" 53 times throughout his Gospel. In comparison, Mark, which was written particularly for the Romans, uses the term "God" only 50 times.

Furthermore, it's clear from reading the New Testament that Jews in Jesus' day had no hesitancy to use the word God. For instance, the unbelieving Jews told Jesus, "We were not born of fornication; we have one Father—God." Likewise, when Jesus healed a blind man on the Sabbath, the Pharisees said, "This Man is not from God, because He does not keep the Sabbath." Again, the Jews told Pilate, "According to our law He ought to die, because He made Himself the Son of God" (Jn. 8:41; 9:16; 19:7).

The truth is that the Mishnah doesn't even forbid Jews to pronounce the Divine name, YHWH, let alone to say the word God. On the contrary, it even encourages a Jew to "greet his fellow with God's name."[5] So Matthew obviously didn't use the term "kingdom of heaven" to avoid offending Jews.

More Counterfeit History

Much of the pseudo history being written by theologians today is done in an effort to promote feminism. The problem is that Jesus never directly taught anything that supports their agenda. So feminists and their theological allies take every situation in Jesus' life involving women and try to turn it into some kind of ground-breaking incident. We saw an example of this with the case of the Samaritan woman mentioned earlier.

In another example, the feminists manage to find something revolutionary in the genealogy of Jesus given in Matthew. The *New International Biblical Commentary* says this about Jesus' genealogy: "[Another] irregularity sets this family record apart from all others: it makes reference to five women. . . This is indeed extraordinary."[6]

The same claim is found in numerous commentaries and study Bibles. However, there is actually nothing extraordinary in Jesus' genealogy including the names of several women. Although it's true that the genealogies in Numbers list only the heads of households, that's not the case for all of the Old Testament genealogies. For example, the genealogies of Abraham, Isaac, Jacob, and Esau all include the names of various women. In fact, more women are named in the genealogy of Esau (Gen. 36) than in the genealogy of Jesus.

Actually, the Old Testament book containing the largest genealogical lists is not Numbers or even Genesis—it's 1 Chronicles. It includes the names of over 50 women in its genealogies. Here are a few examples:

1:50: "His wife's name was Mehetabel the daughter of Matred, the daughter of Mezahab."

2:13-17: "Jesse begot Eliab his firstborn . . . and David the Seventh. Now their sisters were Zeruiah and Abigail. . . . Abigail bore Amasa."

2:18,19: "Caleb the son of Hezron had children by Azubah, his wife, and by Jerioth. . . . When Azubah died, Caleb took Ephrath as his wife, who bore him Hur."

3:1-3: "Now these were the sons of David who were born to him in Hebron: The firstborn was Amnon, by Ahinoam, the Jezreelitess. The second, Daniel, by Abigail, the Carmelitess. The third, Absalom, the son of Maacah, the daughter of Talmai, king of Geshur. The fourth, Adonijah, the son of Haggith. The fifth, Shephatiah, by Abital; the sixth, Ithream, by his wife Eglah.

7:32: "And Heber begot Japhlet, Shomer, Hotham, and their sister Shua."

In short, there was nothing unusual or precedent-setting in Jesus' genealogy including the names of five women.

Detachment from Historic Christianity

I've given some specific examples of historical myths that the theologians have created. But their counterfeit history is merely symptomatic of a much deeper problem: their utter detachment from historic Christianity.

23

Clueless About Historic Christianity

When I say that most theologians are clueless when it comes to historic Christianity, I mean they are totally out of touch with what Christianity originally represented. They don't even remotely think like Christians from the ancient Mediterranean world.

The basis I have for making that charge is that we still have the writings of the early Christians. I'm referring to Christians who lived shortly after the time of the apostles. These were Christians who lived in the same culture as Paul and the other apostles and spoke the same language. In other words, we don't have to guess how the early Christians thought—we can know it from reading their writings. We don't have to guess how they understood the New Testament writings. We can read their writings for ourselves.

I have made early Christianity my special field of study for most of my adult life. And I can say unhesitatingly that no one could read anything written by either today's theologians or by any of the prominent theologians of history and mistake it for something written by the Christians who lived within one or two generations of the apostles.

One of the greatest evidences supporting this is that most modern-day Christians—who have been raised on the teachings of the theologians—find the early Christian writings unexpectedly strange and baffling when they first read them. They're shocked to find that the early Christians knew so little about the cherished doctrines of today's Christianity. "The early Christians got things all mixed up," I often hear. Yet, it never occurs to most modern Christians that the primitive church would find today's Christianity equally baffling and strange. Let me suggest that it's not the unlettered and ordinary Christians who lived so close to the apostles who got things mixed up. Rather, it's today's church and its theologians who have things mixed up.

Christians today vainly imagine that if the apostle John were to walk into one of the second-century churches pastored by Ignatius or Polycarp (men whom he had personally discipled), he would feel totally out of place. They imagine he would find that they held to a different theology, had dissimilar worship practices, reasoned strangely, and even understood his Greek differently.

On the other hand, modern Christians think that if John were to walk into any conservative church today, he would feel right at home. He would find that twenty-first century western Christians think and reason just like first-century Christians living in the Mediterranean world. He would find that today's western Christians worship in the same manner as he did and hold to all the same theological

168 Will the Theologians Please Sit Down

beliefs. He would even find that today's theologians understand *koiné* Greek exactly the way he did.

If you think that's the reality of things, all I can say is dream on!

Holding Fast the Faithful Word

The qualifications for an overseer or bishop in Paul's day required that a man not only be "sober-minded, just, and holy," but also "holding fast the faithful word as he has been taught" (Tit. 1:8,9). In other words, there was no room in the first-century church for brilliant theological innovators. The Christian faith was already complete in Paul's day. The only thing needed was for Christians to hold fast to what they had been taught.

And that's all the second-century Christians claimed to be doing: holding fast to what the apostles had taught them. The only church fathers they knew were Jesus and His apostles. They equated theological innovation with error.

But that's not the way it is today. The men who are held in great esteem by today's church are the theological innovators. The noted church historian, Phillip Schaff, made the following observation: "The men who, next to the apostles, have exerted and still exert through their writings the greatest influence in the Christian Church, as leaders of theological thought, are Augustine, Martin Luther, and John Calvin: all pupils of Paul."[1] Schaff intended his words to be a compliment, but they are really an indictment—an indictment of those theologians and the institutional church that has followed them.

It's interesting that, even in his great admiration for these men, Schaff couldn't bring himself to say that they were pupils of Jesus. Because the simple truth is that they weren't. In fact, they weren't even pupils of Paul. They were re-interpreters of Paul. They took Paul out of context and made him a teacher above his own Master.

But I have to ask: if these three men were merely teaching the historic faith, why are they so prominent? Why have they had such influence? Why are their writings authoritative if they were only passing down what had been taught from the beginning? You see, the whole reason theologians such as Augustine are famous is that they taught things that no one before them had ever taught. If what they taught was merely the historic faith that Christians had always believed, then why can no one produce the writings of any Christians who taught the same things before these theologians did?

When Luther's opponents accused him of creating a new gospel, Luther tried to defend himself by saying, "There was Ambrose, Augustine, and many others who said it before me."[2] Luther was correct in stating that Augustine had preached a similar gospel of easy believism. However, it was a novel teaching in Augustine's day, and few Christians accepted it. Actually, it demonstrates what thin ground Luther was on when he had to depend on Augustine's teachings as his precedent. Augustine lived nearly 400 years after Christ. And as we've seen, Augustine was the epitome of the Christian theological innovator—someone who thought he knew more than everyone who preceded him. And Luther correctly placed himself in the same class as Augustine.

However, Luther was not being truthful in claiming that Ambrose (a fourth-century bishop) had taught the same as Luther. I suppose a person could pull statements here and there from Ambrose's writings to make it look as though he agreed with Luther. However, when a person reads all of what Ambrose said about salvation, it's quite obvious that he didn't even remotely teach Luther's gospel. For example, Ambrose wrote:

> Jesus says, "He that despises me and does not receive my words has one who judges him." Does it seem to you that a person has received Christ's words who has not amended his ways? Undoubtedly not. Rather, he who amends himself receives His word. For this is His word: that everyone should turn back from sin. So, then, of necessity you must either reject this saying of His—or if you cannot deny it, you must accept it. It is also necessary that he who leaves off sinning must keep the commandments of God and renounce his sins."[3]

Who else was Luther able to allege as a proponent of his gospel? The truth is, he couldn't name anyone else. Instead, he simply made the false claim that there were "many others" who taught it. If there actually had been "many others," Luther would have named them. In contrast, when a person holds to the historic faith, he has no trouble citing many faithful Christians who taught the same thing. And he doesn't have to appeal to someone from the class of theologians. He can quote from Christians who lived before the Christian theologians ever arose.

Because the faith received from the apostles was so simple, we should question any new dogmas that go beyond that simple faith. If a continuity of belief can't be traced back to the end of the first century, we can hardly claim that it's the historic faith.

Restoring the Faith?

People who try to defend theologians such as Luther and Calvin soon find that they can't trace the doctrines of such men all the way back to the apostles. These men were not simply defending the historic faith that had always been taught. So their defenders are forced to make the claim that these men were "restoring" the faith. That is, their defenders make the absurd declaration that the men to whom the apostles entrusted leadership of the church quickly lost it all. They lost the crucial theological doctrines of the faith; they lost the essence of what Christianity is all about; and they apparently even lost their knowledge of Greek.

That's a remarkable claim. In other words, the men whom Jesus handpicked to establish and spread His church—whom Scripture calls the "twelve foundations" of the church (Rev. 21:14)—did such a poor job that true Christianity didn't last even one generation after the apostles. That's particularly amazing in light of the fact that Luther's and Calvin's gospels are still going strong nearly five hundred years after those men preached. Are we to believe that mere men have been able to accomplish what the inspired apostles were not?

Jesus promised His apostles, "Lo, I am with you always, even to the end of the age" (Mt. 28:20).

When we embrace the kingdom gospel that Jesus preached, we don't have to invent any fictitious scenarios about a disappearing church. Kingdom Christians have been around from the beginning, and they are still around today. They don't have to invent fake scenarios, and they don't have to be theological innovators.

The kingdom gospel was the mainline, predominant gospel in the second and third centuries. There are plenty of witnesses to that fact. Although the theologians shoved the kingdom gospel out of the mainstream of institutional Christianity in the fourth century, there were still plenty of kingdom Christians around.* Kingdom Christians have been the persecuted or marginalized minority ever since the fourth century, but they have never disappeared. There are no famous theologians connected to kingdom Christianity, and there never will be. The kingdom gospel can be traced back to the beginning because it's truly the historic faith.

---

* As I mentioned earlier, by the term "kingdom Christian," I'm referring to Christians who recognize the centrality of the kingdom of God in this present life. They realize that God's kingdom cannot be joined to any of the kingdoms of this world. These are also Christians who, through the grace of God, are committed to living by Jesus' teachings—particularly His teachings in the Sermon on the Mount.

24

The Fruit of the Theologians

In His parable of the vine, Jesus explained how Christianity works: "I am the true vine, and My Father is the vinedresser. Every branch in Me that does not bear fruit He takes away; and every branch that bears fruit He prunes, that it may bear more fruit" (Jn. 15:1,2).

Just as the Jewish theologians imagined they could please God without producing godly fruit, so Christian theologians have devised numerous systems that offer eternal life without the need to bear kingdom fruit.

Luther believed that the primary problem with the Catholic Church was that Catholics were trying to work their way to heaven. Actually, the real problem with the Catholic Church of Luther's day was that it offered heaven without the necessity of bearing Christ's fruit. Catholics imagined that they could somehow receive eternal life by going on pilgrimages, viewing relics, attending Mass, and obtaining papal indulgences. Whether a person labels such things as works or counterfeit grace, one thing is for sure: they're not kingdom fruit.

174 Will the Theologians Please Sit Down

And what did Luther offer in place of the Catholic system of entering heaven without bearing fruit? He offered a Protestant system of gaining heaven without bearing fruit. Instead of pilgrimages and indulgences, Luther offered theological doctrine. Just give mental assent to the doctrine of salvation by faith alone, and you will be saved. No fruit needed.

Ungodly Fruit

Actually, Luther thought that godly fruit would automatically follow once a person embraced his gospel. But somehow that fruit never came. Even Schaff, who was an ardent admirer of Luther and a firm believer in the Reformer, was forced to admit:

> The fact is undeniable that the Reformation in Germany was accompanied and followed by antinomian tendencies and a degeneracy of public morals. It rests not only on the hostile testimonies of Romanists and separatists, but Luther and Melanchthon themselves often bitterly complained in their later years of the abuse of the liberty of the gospel and the sad state of morals in Wittenberg and throughout Saxony.[1]

Luther himself wrote, "Since our doctrines have been preached, the world has grown steadily worse, always more godless and shameless, and men more avaricious and unchaste than under the Papacy. Everywhere are only greed, immoderate desires, lewdness, shameful disorder and hideous passions."[2]

In a letter to his wife near the end of his life, Luther lamented about the degenerate morals of Wittenberg—the city where Luther lived and where the Reformation had begun: "As things are run in Wittenberg, perhaps the people there will acquire not only the dance of St. Vitus or St. John, but the dance of the beggars or the dance of Beelzebub, since they have started to bare women and maidens in front and back, and there is no one who punishes or objects. In addition, the Word of God is being mocked. Away from this Sodom! . . . I am tired of this city and do not wish to return."[3]

Philip Melanchthon, Luther's right-hand man and his successor, confessed: "The morals of the people become worse. Luxury, licentiousness and boldness are steadily increasing."[4] The truth is that Lutheran Germany produced no more kingdom fruit than had Catholic Germany. In fact, it produced even less. Catholic Germany gave the world centuries of wars. Lutheran Germany did the same, culminating with World War II. As Jesus said, "A good tree cannot bear bad fruit, nor can a bad tree bear good fruit" (Mt. 7:18). Both Catholic and Lutheran Germany were rotten trees.

Maybe you're thinking, "Well, perhaps the problem is that most of the people of Lutheran Germany never embraced Reformation theology. Why don't you point instead to the personal fruit of the Reformers themselves." Well, actually the people of Lutheran Germany *did* embrace Reformation theology. The problem is that they never embraced Christ. After all, it was Luther himself who advised Melanchthon, "Sin boldly."[5] Nevertheless, let's look at the personal fruit of the Reformers themselves.

The Personal Fruit of the Reformers

Luther once said that there is no worse heresy than for a Christian to believe that he is good enough to deserve salvation. To be sure, that is a major theological error. However, I can think of several heresies that are far, far worse. A much worse heresy is murdering others in the name of Christ and imagining that God is pleased with it.

Based on the hearty approval of Augustine, the Catholic Church had been torturing and murdering Christians, Jews, and Muslims in the name of Christ for centuries. If there was any one thing we could expect that a true reformation would bring about, it would be an end to such a monstrous sin and blasphemy against Christ. But the Reformation accomplished no such thing. In fact, all the major Reformers had blood stains on their hands.

The Swiss Reformer, Zwingli, personally ordered the deaths of those innocent Christians who preached and practiced a more radical reformation than he wanted to follow. Calvin personally ordered the torture and death of many who opposed his reformation in Geneva. He had Michael Servetus arrested and put to death for no other reason than that Servetus held to an erroneous view of the Trinity. Calvin's right-hand man, William Farel, personally led Servetus to the stake where he was burned alive, and he watched with satisfaction as Servetus writhed in pain.

Philip Melanchthon, Luther's successor in Germany, heartily approved of Servetus' murder and even wrote a congratulatory letter to Calvin. In his letter, Melanchthon said, "Reverend sir and dearest brother, I have read your work in which you have lucidly refuted the horrible blasphemies of Servetus, and I thank the Son of God, who has been the arbiter of this your contest. The church, both now and in

all generations, owes and I owe you a debt of grati-
tude. I entirely assent to your judgment. And I say,
too, that your magistrates did right in that, after
solemn trial, they put the blasphemer to death."[6]

In the previous chapter, I quoted from Schaff,
who referred to Luther and Calvin as "pupils of
Paul." All I can say is that if these men and their
associates were pupils of Paul, they were pupils of
the unconverted Paul who heartily approved of the
stoning of Stephen.

Luther's Own Fruit

One only has to read the writings of Luther for
himself to see that the spirit driving this Reformer
was something other than the spirit of Christ.
Erasmus correctly assessed Luther when he wrote:

> Sound human reason teaches me that a man cannot
> honestly further the cause of God who excites so great
> an uproar in the world and finds delight in abuse and
> sarcasm—and cannot have enough of them. Such an
> amount of arrogance as we have never seen surpassed
> cannot possibly be without some folly. And such a
> boisterous individual is not at all in harmony with the
> apostolic spirit.[7]

In chapter 15, we saw some examples of the abuse,
sarcasm, and arrogance of which Erasmus spoke.
Over and over again, Luther launched into violent
tirades against his opponents, heaping scorn and
ridicule upon them and assailing them with the
harshest invectives. He called Erasmus the "enemy
to true religion," the "open adversary of Christ," an
"accursed wretch," and "the vilest miscreant that
ever disgraced the earth."[8] Luther once said, "Whenever I pray, I pray a curse upon Erasmus."[9] Upon

Erasmus' death, Luther haughtily pronounced him eternally lost.[10]

However, it wasn't only Erasmus, the Pope, and the Anabaptists that Luther viciously assailed. He even savagely attacked many of his fellow Reformers, such as Zwingli. He did this because they viewed the bread and wine in communion as symbols, whereas Luther believed that Christ was truly present in some supernatural sense in the bread and wine. Luther called these men blasphemers, hypocrites, cowards, liars, heretics, soul murderers, and sinners unto death.[11] He gloated over Zwingli's death, calling it an act of judgment from God.[12] He said, "I would much rather be torn to pieces and burned a hundred times than be of one mind and will with Schwenkfeld [and] Zwingli."[13]

However, Luther's venom wasn't reserved just for his theological rivals. When the peasants rose up against the cruel and ungodly treatment they received at the hands of the Lutheran nobility, Luther urged the nobles to slaughter the peasants without mercy. The nobles wasted no time in following Luther's directive, killing up to 100,000 peasants.[14] Years later, Luther shamelessly boasted, "I, Martin Luther, slew all the peasants in the rebellion, for I said that they should be slain. All their blood is upon my head. But I cast it on the Lord God, who commanded me to speak in this way!"[15]

At the beginning of the Reformation, Luther was so certain that he had restored original Christianity, he believed the Jews would now finally come to Christ. When his imaginings failed to materialize, Luther turned against the Jews with fury. In 1543,

Luther penned a work entitled *The Jews and Their Lies.* He addressed the work to the German princes, urging them to take violent measures against the Jews. He wrote:

> What shall we Christians do with this rejected and condemned people, the Jews? We dare not tolerate their conduct, now that we are aware of their lying and blaspheming. If we do, we become sharers in their lies, cursing and blasphemy. I shall give you my sincere advice:
>
> First, set fire to their synagogues or schools and bury and cover with dirt whatever will not burn, so that no man will ever again see a stone or cinder of them. This is to be done in honor of our Lord and of Christendom, so that God might see that we are Christians.
>
> Second, I advise that their houses also be razed and destroyed. This will bring home to them the fact that they are not masters in our country, as they boast. Third, I advise that all their prayer books and Talmudic writings be taken from them. Fourth, I advise that their rabbis be forbidden to teach on pain of loss of life and limb.
>
> Fifth, I advise that safe-conduct on the highways be abolished completely for the Jews. For they have no business in the countryside, since they are not lords, officials, tradesmen, or the like. Let them stay at home. For you must not and cannot protect them unless you wish to become participants in their abominations in the sight of God.
>
> Sixth, I advise that charging interest be prohibited to them, and that all cash and treasure of silver and gold be taken from them and put aside for safe-keeping. Through usury, they have stolen and robbed from *us* all they possess.

Seventh, I recommend putting a flail, an ax, a hoe, a spade, a distaff, or a spindle into the hands of young, strong Jews and Jewesses and letting them earn their bread in the sweat of their brow. For it is not fitting that they should let us accursed Gentiles toil in the sweat of our faces while they, the holy people, idle away their time behind the stove, feasting and passing gas*, and on top of all, boasting blasphemously of their lordship over the Christians by means of our sweat. No, we should toss out these lazy rogues by the seat of their pants.

Finally, let us emulate the common sense of other nations such as France, Spain, and Bohemia and eject them forever from the country.[16]

I see, the way we Christians should conduct ourselves is to burn down all the synagogues and persecute the Jews. We should do this "so that God might see that we are Christians." And Luther called himself a Christian *teacher*? Why, he didn't understand the most elementary things about the kingdom of God.

Luther's murderous and hate-filled spirit was the fruit of his own teaching. He vainly imagined: "No sin can separate us from Him, even if we were to kill or commit adultery thousands of times each day. Do you think such an exalted Lamb paid merely a small price with a meager sacrifice for our sins?"[17] In Luther's mind, the only thing that can separate us from God is to hold to a wrong theology. God is more interested in our theology than in our fruit.

---

* I have softened Luther's actual language here, as it is too vulgar to print.

This is not the thinking of Jesus, but the thinking of a man who was a total stranger to the kingdom of God. This is the thinking of Doctrianity—not Christianity.

As I write this chapter, a drama has just unfolded in the news concerning a man named George Sodini, age 48. He calmly walked into a Pittsburg gym and began randomly shooting women in an aerobics exercise class. He killed three women and seriously wounded nine more before taking his own life.

But George Sodini was no ordinary mass murderer. He was a product of Luther's easy believism, the epitome of someone who took seriously Luther's advice to "sin boldly." Before committing his heinous crime, George Sodini wrote an explanation of why he was doing it—a memorandum to be read after he died. In it he said:

> "Soon I will see God and Jesus. At least that is what I was told. Eternal life does NOT depend on works. If it did, we will all be in hell. Christ paid for EVERY sin, so how can I or you be judged BY GOD for a sin when the penalty was ALREADY paid. People judge but that does not matter. I was reading the Bible and *The Integrity of God* beginning yesterday, because soon I will see them."[18]

Like many others, George Sodini belonged to a religion. But his religion was not Christianity. It was Doctrianity. He "knew" he was going straight to heaven after committing his horrible crime, for he held to the "right" doctrine.

25

To Which Religion Do *You* Belong?

Now, let me ask *you* a question. To which religion do you belong: Christianity or Doctrianity? Unless you're an unusual person, I'm sure your answer is Christianity. I've never met a person yet who will acknowledge that his religion is really Doctrianity.

So let me ask you a different question: Suppose you were standing at the gates of heaven and Jesus asked you, "Why should I let you in?" What would your answer be?

Perhaps you recognize my question as being the same question that Christians frequently ask non-believers when witnessing to them. And no doubt you have a ready answer. So let's talk about your answer for a moment. It reveals a lot about yourself and your religion.

First of all, does your answer focus on theology or fruit? The persons who use that question in evangelism are normally looking for a theological answer. The right answer is supposedly: "You should let me in because I believed in you alone for my salvation and put no trust in my own works."

However, on Judgment Day, Jesus is going to look for fruit, not theological answers. He's already made that crystal clear:

When the Son of Man comes in His glory, and all the holy angels with Him, then He will sit on the throne of His glory. All the nations will be gathered before Him, and He will separate them one from another, as a shepherd divides *his* sheep from the goats. And He will set the sheep on His right hand, but the goats on the left. Then the King will say to those on His right hand, "Come, you blessed of My Father, inherit the kingdom prepared for you from the foundation of the world: for I was hungry and you gave Me food; I was thirsty and you gave Me drink; I was a stranger and you took Me in; I *was* naked and you clothed Me; I was sick and you visited Me; I was in prison and you came to Me."

Then the righteous will answer Him, saying, "Lord, when did we see You hungry and feed *You,* or thirsty and give *You* drink? When did we see You a stranger and take *You* in, or naked and clothe *You?* Or when did we see You sick, or in prison, and come to You?" And the King will answer and say to them, "Assuredly, I say to you, inasmuch as you did *it* to one of the least of these My brethren, you did *it* to Me."

Then He will also say to those on the left hand, "Depart from Me, you cursed, into the everlasting fire prepared for the devil and his angels: for I was hungry and you gave Me no food; I was thirsty and you gave Me no drink; I was a stranger and you did not take Me in, naked and you did not clothe Me, sick and in prison and you did not visit Me." Then they also will answer Him, saying, "Lord, when did we see You hungry or thirsty or a stranger or naked or sick or in prison, and did not minister to

You?" Then He will answer them, saying, "Assuredly, I say to you, inasmuch as you did not do *it* to one of the least of these, you did not do *it* to Me." And these will go away into everlasting punishment, but the righteous into eternal life (Mt. 25:31–46).

So Jesus isn't going to be looking for correct theological answers on Judgment Day. He's going to be looking for fruit. Theologians may assure us that we can enter eternal life without fruit, but Jesus says otherwise. And His opinion is the only one that counts.

Is This "Works Salvation"?

Does this mean that Jesus taught a "works salvation"? Not if by "works salvation," you mean a salvation that we earn by our own efforts or merits. In His parable of the vine, Jesus explained: "Abide in Me, and I in you. As the branch cannot bear fruit of itself, unless it abides in the vine, neither can you, unless you abide in Me. I am the vine, you are the branches. He who abides in Me, and I in him, bears much fruit; for without Me you can do nothing" (Jn. 15:4,5).

So we can never be "good enough" on our own strength to be saved. A person who truly maintains an obedient love-faith relationship with Jesus Christ, will always be a person who realizes how utterly dependent he is on God's grace for his salvation. As Jesus said, "Without Me you can do nothing." I know that I would be absolutely nowhere without God's amazing grace.

Martin Luther was correct in teaching that we cannot earn our way into heaven. The problem is that Luther acted as though the main point of Jesus' parable of the vine was that we can do nothing without Him. That is certainly one of the points of His parable, and it is surely a vital truth. However, the point of the parable is that we *must* produce fruit if we're going to remain on the vine and inherit eternal life.

Luther confused the means with the end. The end is fruit. The means is the power that comes from an abiding relationship with Jesus Christ.

Knowledge Is Not Fruit

By way of illustration, imagine John Smith, a homeowner living in the early 1950s. For years, John has struggled trying to mow his yard with an old-fashioned push reel mower powered solely through human muscle. However, one day John discovers that there are gasoline-powered, self-propelled mowers. With such mowers, the homeowner's primary job is to guide the mower as he walks behind it. Filled with amazement, John immediately goes out and buys a power mower. John is so excited in learning that a person can mow his yard without having to depend on his own strength that he immediately tells the good news to his neighbors. They, too, go out and buy power mowers.

However, John and his neighbors never actually mow their yards with their newly discovered mowers. They spend lots of time showing their mowers to others and explaining that a person can mow his yard without having to depend on his own strength. That's because all the power comes from the gasoline engine. But none of these people ever mow their yards, and soon their lawns are covered with foot-high grass and weeds.

It was the same way with Luther and most of the theologians of the Reformation. They rejoiced to discover that without Christ we can do nothing. They exulted in the knowledge that the power to live the Christian life comes through Jesus. They eagerly spread the good news about that. But they ignored what Jesus said about producing fruit.

Understanding how a power mower works does not get a lawn mowed. Likewise, understanding how the Vine works does not in itself produce fruit. What matters is whether or not we actually produce fruit—not whether we can correctly explain how the whole process works.

"Without Me you can do nothing" does not mean: "There is no role you play in producing fruit." The whole point of Jesus' parable of the vine is that we must produce fruit or else be cut off of the vine. If fruit comes automatically, there would be no point to Jesus' parable.

So what role do we play? Jesus explains, "As the branch cannot bear fruit of itself, unless it abides in the vine, neither can you, unless you abide in Me" (Jn. 15:4). So the role we play is to abide in Christ Jesus.

At first glance, that may sound as though we play only a passive role in producing fruit. We just need to abide in Jesus. But what does it mean to abide? Other translations use more familiar terms such as "remain in Me," "dwell in Me," "live in Me," or "remain united to Me."[1] And what is required to live in Christ or remain united to Him? He Himself clarifies this at the end of His parable when He says, "If you keep My commandments, you will abide in My love" (Jn. 15:10).

So to abide or dwell in Christ, we must keep His commandments. Or to put it another way, to abide in Jesus we must truly love Him. And if we truly love Him, we will keep His commandments. To enter heaven, we must maintain an obedient love-faith relationship with Jesus. As William Law expressed it: "The one true proof that we are living members of Christ's church on earth, is nothing else but our having the inward nature and the outward behavior that Christ manifested to the world."[2]

However, theologians want to convince us that what matters most to God is our doctrines. They've convinced millions of professing Christians that we can't believe what Jesus said about Judgment Day. According to them, He's not going to be looking for kingdom fruit. Rather He's going to be looking for the right theological answers. The theologians certainly did a good job of convincing George Sodini, the mass-murderer, of that.

Like their predecessors, the scribes and Pharisees, Christian theologians have consistently missed the essence of God's message to mankind. Rather than shedding light on God's Word, they have more often hidden it in darkness with their theological books, study Bibles, and commentaries. They nullify most of Christ's commandments by using language bullying, counterfeit history, and the claim that they truly know the historic faith.

Throw Off the Shackles

It's time for those who truly love Jesus Christ to throw off the shackles of Doctrianity. By that, I don't mean that we need to throw away the theological doctrines of the historic faith. By no means.

Rather, it's time to let Jesus speak through the pages of the Gospels, without filtering His teachings through the denials, mental gymnastics, and reinterpretations of the theologians. It's time for the children of the kingdom to stand up for Jesus and the gospel He preached. And it's time for the theologians to sit down.

Notes

CH. 1: "DOCTRIANITY" VERSUS CHRISTIANITY

1. This is a dramatized narration of a true story, witnessed by court records and recorded in *Quellen zur Geschichte der Wiedertüufer, 1. Band Herzogtum Württemberg,* ed. Gustav Bossert (Leipzig, 1930), 216 f.

CH. 2: THE FIRST THEOLOGIANS

1. "Rabbi." *Wikipedia, The Free Encyclopedia.* 19 Mar 2009, 08:42 UTC. http://en.wikipedia.org.
2. Shabbat 11:3. *The Mishnah,* trans. Jacob Neusner (New Haven: Yale University Press, 1988), 193.
3. *Ibid.*

CH. 4: HOW JESUS OVERTURNED THE THEOLOGIANS

1. These alternate readings are from *The New American Bible* (New York: P. J. Kennedy & Sons, 1970) and *The Holy Bible, New International Version* (Grand Rapids: The Zondervan Corporation, 1978), respectively.

CH. 5: THE KINGDOM OF CHILDREN

1. Justin Martyr, *Address to the Greeks,* ch. 35. *The Ante-Nicene Fathers,* ed. Alexander Roberts and James Donaldson, vol. 1 (Peabody, MA: Hendrickson Publishers, Inc., 1996), 288.
2. Tatian, *Address to the Greeks,* ch. 29. *ANF,* vol. 2, 77.
3. Origen, *Against Celsus,* bk. 6, ch. 2. *ANF,* vol. 4, 573.
4. Origen, *Against Celsus,* bk. 7, ch. 59. *ANF,* vol. 4, 634.
5. Origen, *Against Celsus,* bk. 7, ch. 60. *ANF,* vol. 4, 635.
6. Arnobius *Against the Nations,* bk. 1, ch. 58,59. *ANF,* vol. 6, 429,430.

CH. 7: THE NEXT GENERATION AFTER THE APOSTLES

1. For example, see Eusebius, *Ecclesiastical History,* bk. 3, ch. 24.
2. Justin Martyr, *First Apology,* ch. 14. *ANF,* vol. 1, 167.

190 Will the Theologians Please Sit Down

3. Tertullian, *On the Veiling of Virgins*, ch. 1. *ANF*, vol. 4, 27.
4. Richard Hooker, "A Learned Discourse of Justification," quoted in *New World Encyclopedia*, 11 Apr 2009, http://www.newworldencyclopedia.org/ entry/Richard_ Hooker.

CH. 9: THE FIRST THEOLOGICAL BRAWL
1. Eusebius, *Life of Constantine*, bk. 2, ch. 69.

CH. 10: THE MAJOR TURNING POINT IN CHRISTIAN HISTORY
1. *The Nicene and Post-Nicene Fathers, Second Series*, ed. Philip Schaff and Henry Wace, vol. 14 (Peabody, MA: Hendrickson Publishers, Inc., 1996), 3.
2. For example, *ousia* is translated as "goods" or "possessions" in Luke 15:12, 13: "And the younger of them said to his father, 'Father, give me the portion of *goods* that falls to me. So he divided to them his livelihood. And not many days after, the younger son gathered all together, journeyed to a far country, and there wasted his *possessions* with prodigal living."

CH. 12: WHAT HAPPENED WHILE THE THEOLOGIANS WRANGLED
1. Canon 12 of the Nicene Canons states: "As many as were called by grace and displayed the first zeal, having cast aside their military girdles, but afterwards returned like dogs to their own vomit (so that some spent money and by means of gifts regained their military stations), let these, after they have passed the space of three years as hearers [i.e., they are excommunicated] be for ten years prostrators." *The Nicene and Post-Nicene Fathers, Second Series*, vol. 14, 27.
2. Augustine, *Reply to Faustus*, bk. 22, ch. 76. *The Nicene and Post-Nicene Fathers, First Series*, ed. Philip Schaff, vol. 4, 301.
3. *Ibid.*, ch. 74.
4. *Ibid.*, ch. 75.

CH. 13: WHAT ELSE HAPPENED BECAUSE OF NICAEA
1. Augustine, *Heresies* 56. Quotation can be found at http://www.catholic.com/library/Mary_Ever_Virgin.asp.

2. Augustine, *Sermons* 186:1. Quotation can be found at http://www.catholic.com/library/Mary_Ever_Virgin.asp.
3. Augustine, *On Nature and Grace*, ch. 42.
4. Augustine, *Our Lord's Sermon on the Mount*, bk. 1, ch. 17. *The Nicene and Post-Nicene Fathers, First Series*, vol. 6, 22.
5. Augustine, *Lord's Sermon on the Mount*, bk. 1, ch. 20.

CH. 14: THE PROBLEM WITH DOCTRIANITY
1. William Law, *You Will Receive Power* (New Kensington, Pa: Whitaker House, 1997), 57.

CH. 15: LUTHER—THEOLOGIAN IN SHEEP'S CLOTHING
1. Law, 29, 30.
2. Martin Luther, "Preface to New Testament," *Works of Martin Luther*, vol. 6 (Grand Rapids: Baker Book House, 1982), 439.
3. Luther, "Preface to Hebrews," *Works*, vol. 6, 476.
4. Luther, "An Open Letter on Translating," quoted from Project Guttenberg, 31 Aug 2009, http://infomotions.com/etexts/gutenberg/dirs/etext95/ltran11.txt.
5. Law, 30.
6. For example, Menno Simons, a prominent Anabaptist, wrote: "True evangelical faith is of such a nature that it cannot lie dormant, but manifests itself in all righteousness and works of love; it dies unto flesh and blood; destroys all forbidden lusts and desires; cordially seeks, serves and fears God; clothes the naked; feeds the hungry; consoles the afflicted; shelters the miserable; aids and consoles all the oppressed; returns good for evil; serves those who injure it; prays for those who persecute it; teaches, admonishes and reproves with the Word of the Lord; seeks that which is lost; binds up that which is wounded; heals that which is diseased and saves that which is sound." *Complete Writings of Menno Simons*, trans. Leonard Verduin (Scottsdale, Pa: Herald Press, 1956), 307.
7. Roland Bainton, *The Reformation of the Sixteenth Century* (Boston: Beacon Press, 1952), 101.
8. Bainton, 101, 102.
9. Martin Luther, quoted in Johannes Janssen, *Geschichte des deutschen Volkes seit dem Ausgang des Mittelalters* (8 vols.,

Freiburg, 1878-1894). This quotation can be found in
English in "Why Did the Protestant Reformers Have No
Toleration for Anyone After the Reformation?" at
http://answers.yahoo.com/ question/index?qid=
20080727084322AAOUDcs.
10. *Ibid.*
11. Martin Luther, "Commentary on 82nd Psalm," *Works of
Martin Luther*, vol. 4, 309-311.

CH. 16: HOW THE THEOLOGIANS ENTRENCHED
THEMSELVES
1. Martin Luther, "Commentary on 82nd Psalm," 312, 313.
2. Luther, *Preface to the New Testament.*
3. For example, see the Geneva Bible notes for Mt. 5:19 and
Mt. 7:24.

CH. 17: COMMENTARIES THAT MUFFLE GOD'S
WORD
1. John Calvin, *Calvin's Commentaries*, trans. Joseph
Haroutunian, Christian Classics Ethereal Library, 20 Apr
2009, http:// http://www.ccel.org/ccel/calvin/calcom31.html
2. *Ibid.*
3. *Ibid.*

CH. 18: LEARNING TO STAND UP TO THEOLOGICAL
BULLIES
1. "Bullying." *Wikipedia, The Free Encyclopedia.* 21 Apr 2009,
http://en.wikipedia.org/wiki/Bullying.
2. "The Serial Bully," www.bullyonline.org/workbully/
serial.htm

CH. 19: EXPOSING THE BLINDNESS OF
THEOLOGIANS
1. www.cnn.com/2009/ TECH/ 06/09/million.words/
index.html.
2. Webster's New World College Dictionary, Third Edition,
s.v. "Literal."
3. F. C. Conybeare and St. George Stock, *Grammar of
Septuagint Greek*, (Peabody, MA: Hendrickson Publishers,
Inc., 1995), 20. Quotation has been slightly modernized.

4. "God's Love—Agape,"http://www.shalomindia.com/
   agape.php.
5. This is called 2 Kings in the LXX.

CH. 20: COUNTERFEIT HISTORY
1. John Calvin, *Calvin's Commentaries.*
2. William Burkitt, *Expository Notes with Practical
   Observations on the New Testament*, reproduced in
   SwordSearcher [CD-ROM].
3. Robert Jameison, A. R. Faucett, and David Brown,
   Commentary Critical and Explanatory on the Whole Bible,
   reproduced in Bible Explorer 4.0 (Austin: WORDSearch,
   2006).
4. *A Commentary on the Whole Bible*, ed. J. R. Dummelow
   (New York: The Macmillan Co., 1942), 909.
5. "Throughout Greece and certain of its barbaric provinces,
   the majority of churches keep their virgins covered. There
   are places, too, beneath this African sky where this practice
   obtains; lest any ascribe the custom to Greek or barbarian
   Gentilehood." Tertullian, *On the Veiling of Virgins*, ch. 2.
   ANF, vol. 4, 28.
6. "For some, with their turbans and woolen bands, do not *veil*
   their head, but bind it up; protected, indeed, in front, but
   where the head properly lies, bare. Others are to a certain
   extent covered over the region of the brain with linen coifs
   of small dimensions. . . . But how severe a chastisement will
   they likewise deserve, who, amid the recital of the Psalms
   and at any mention of the name of God, continue uncovered; who even when about to spend time in prayer itself,
   with the utmost readiness place a fringe, or a tuft, or any
   thread whatever on the crown of their heads, and suppose
   themselves to be covered?" Tertullian, *On the Veiling of
   Virgins*, ch. 17. *ANF*, vol. 4, 37.

   The fact that Christian sisters wore a cloth veil when praying is corroborated by the many paintings in the catacombs.

CH. 21: WHEN FICTION IS PRESENTED AS FACT
1. Adam Clarke, *Adam Clarke's Bible Commentary*, 05 June
   2009, http://www.godrules.net/library/clarke/
   clarke1cor11.htm.
2. Shabbat 6.5,6.6. *The Mishnah*, 186.

3. Tertullian, *De Corona*, ch. 4. *ANF,* vol. 3, 95.
4. Matthew Henry, *Matthew Henry's Commentary on the Whole Bible*, reproduced in SwordSearcher [CD-ROM].
5. "Arabia's heathen females will be your judges, who cover not only the head, but the face also." Tertullian, *On the Veiling of Virgins*, ch. 17. *ANF*, vol. 4, 37.
6. For example, see *The New Testament World in Pictures* (Nashville: Broadman Press, 1987).
7. William Barclay, *The Letters to the Corinthians* (Philadelphia: Westminster Press, 1975), 99.
8. Strabo, *Geography*, 8.6.20-23.
9. Strabo, 8.6.23.
10. *Ibid.*

CH. 22: MEN DIDN'T TALK TO WOMEN—AND OTHER LIES

1. 1 Kings 17:8-24.
2. Robert H. Mounce, *New International Biblical Commentary on Matthew* (Peabody, MA: Hendrickson Publishers, 1991), 22.
3. For example, Papias indicated that Matthew had written his Gospel particularly for the Jews. *ANF*, vol. 1, 155.
4. "The Name of G-d," http://www.jewfaq.org/name.htm.
5. Berakhot 9:5.
6. Robert H. Mounce, 8.

CH. 23: CLUELESS ABOUT HISTORIC CHRISTIANITY

1. Philip Schaff, *History of the Christian Church*, 2nd ed., vol. 7 (Grand Rapids: Wm. B. Eerdmans Publishing Co., 1985), 736.
2. Martin Luther, "An Open Letter on Translating," trans. Gary Mann from: "Sendbrief von Dolmetschen" in *Dr. Martin Luthers Werke* (Weimar: Hermann Boehlaus Nachfolger, 1909), Band 30, Teil II, 632-646.
3. Ambrose, *Concerning Repentance*, bk. 1, ch. 55-56. *The Nicene and Post-Nicene Fathers, Second Series*, vol. 10, 338.

CHAPTER 24: THE FRUIT OF THE THEOLOGIANS

1. Philip Schaff, 23.
2. Johann Joseph von Dollinger, *The Reformation*, vol. 1, 289. Quoted in Schaff.

3. Martin Luther, *Letter 312 To Mrs. Martin Luther* [Zeitz,] (1 July 28, 1545 http://beggarsallreformation.blogspot.com /2009/04/luther-on-wittenberg-away-from-this.html.
4. Dollinger, 97.
5. Martin Luther, *Letter to Melanchthon, Letter 99* (Aug. 1, 1521).
6. Phillip Melanchthon, as quoted by Philip Schaff, *History*, vol. 7, 62.
7. Dollinger, 97.
8. From *Table Talk*, published by the Lutheran Publication Society.
9. *Ibid.*
10. *Ibid.*
11. Schaff, 656.
12. *Ibid.*
13. *Ibid.*
14. "Peasants' War," *Wikipedia, The Free Encyclopedia.* 22 Apr 2009, 09: 22 UTC. http://en.wikipedia.org.
15. Dollinger, 96.
16. Martin Luther, *The Jews and Their Lies.*
17. Martin Luther, *Letter to Melanchthon, Letter 99* (Aug. 1, 1521).
18. Blog of George Sodini. http://raincoaster.com/2009/08/05/ george-sodinis-blog-the-plan, 3 Sept 2009.

CH. 25: TO WHICH RELIGION DO YOU BELONG?

1. These are the renderings used in the *James Moffat Translation*, *The New English Bible*, *The New American Bible*, and the *Twentieth Century New Testament*.
2. Law, 151.

Will the Real Heretics Please Stand Up

David Bercot

Sex and money scandals. An exploding divorce rate. Drug-addicted youths. And an ever-growing worldliness. Today's church is fighting battles on all fronts. And we seem to be losing these battles to the relentlessly encroaching world. Perhaps the answers to our problems are not in the present, but in the past. Because there was a time when Christians were able to stand up to the world.

The author takes you on an engrossing journey back to that time—back to the end of the first century. Here is an inspiring account of what Christians believed and practiced at the close of the age of the apostles—and how the church eventually lost the Christianity of that time.

192 pp. Paperback. $9.95

Scroll Publishing Co., P. O. Box 122
Amberson, PA 17210 • (717) 349-7033
www.scrollpublishing.com

The Kingdom That Turned the World Upside Down

David Bercot

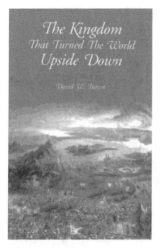

The theme of Jesus' message was the kingdom of God. But the message of the kingdom is almost totally missing from the gospel that's preached today. As a result, a lot of Christians don't realize that the kingdom of God is a present reality on earth. In fact, they don't even know what the kingdom of God is. Consequently, they never make the kingdom commitment that Christ requires.

In *The Kingdom That Turned the World Upside Down,* David Bercot takes the reader back to Jesus' teachings of the kingdom—teachings that have too often been forgotten. Bercot describes the radically new laws of the kingdom and its upside-down values. This book will challenge you to the core in your Christian walk!

282 pp. Paperback. $9.95

www.scrollpublishing.com • (717) 349-7033
P. O. Box 122 • Amberson, PA 17210

To capture the spirit of primitive
Christianity, we recommend:

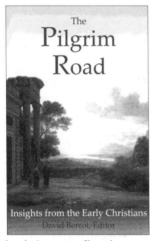

The
Pilgrim
Road

The Pilgrim Road is a unique devotional book that collects together the best insights, reflections, and practical counsel of the early Christians. During the 2nd and 3rd centuries A.D., Christianity was an illegal, persecuted religion throughout most of the civilized world. In many ways, this was a blessing. Persecution culled out superficial Christians and those who were not willing to make sacrifices for Christ.

The passionate Christianity of those early centuries can bless today's Christians as well. That's because the spiritual pilgrims of those early centuries have left us a rich legacy of vibrant writings that provide keen insight on how to walk down the pilgrim road. 179 pp. Paperback. $8.95

198

We Don't Speak Great Things— We Live Them

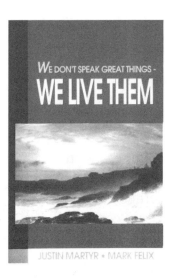

Here are two of the best early Christian writings under one cover: Mark Felix's *Octavius* and Justin Martyr's *First Apology*.

Justin Martyr's *First Apology* is the oldest Christian apology still in existence in its entirety. It gives readers a window into the primitive church, enabling them to witness first hand what Christianity was like in the 2nd century. In it, Justin Martyr describes a typical baptism and church service in his day (c. A.D. 150).

Octavius is written as a debate between a pagan and a Christian. It takes a look at Christianity from both the pagan and Christian viewpoints. It is arguably the greatest and most readable apologetic work produced by the early church. It challenges us all to return to the love and the faith of the early Christians. 160 pp. Paperback. $7.95

www.scrollpublishing.com • (717) 349-7033

P. O. Box 122 • Amberson, PA 17210

Free Catalog

We encourage you to see our entire collection of family books and audio recordings, together with books on committed Christian discipleship. All of the books, teaching CDs, and music we carry can be seen on our website at www.scrollpublishing.com. Or, you may contact us to receive our free catalog.

Scroll Publishing Co.
www.scrollpublishing.com

P. O. Box 122
Amberson, PA 17210
(717) 349-7033

Fax (717) 349-7558
e-mail: customerservice@scrollpublishing.com